Business Letters

Published by
Lotus Press Publishers & Distributors

Business Letters

Nimmoo Kinger

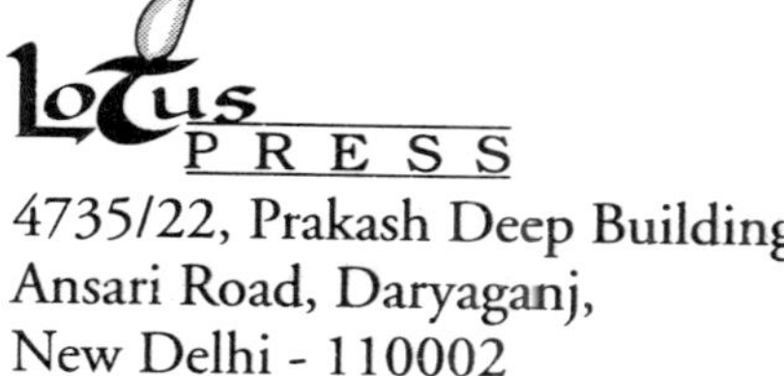

4735/22, Prakash Deep Building,
Ansari Road, Daryaganj,
New Delhi - 110002

Lotus Press Publishers & Distributors
Unit No.220, 2nd Floor, 4735/22, Prakash Deep Building,
Ansari Road, Daryaganj, New Delhi- 110002
Ph:- 32903912, 23280047, 098118-38000
Email : lotuspress1984@gmail.com
Visit us : www.lotuspress.co.in

Business Letters

ISBN : 81-89093-73-8

Printed & Published by **: Lotus Press Publishers & Distributors,** New Delhi- 2

PREFACE

Business correspondence is a major form of communication in the business world and requires certain professional skills to be effective. Over the years, business correspondence has developed and retained a formal structure governed by the need for personal relationship and professional courtesy.

In response to the expansion of the media of communication, a section on electronic mail or e-mail, as it is popularly called, has been included. Correspondence by electronic means in general follows the same norms of courtesy and preciseness. The format, however, is slightly different from that of a regular letter. Specifically, one needs to guard against a tendency to treat e-mail carelessly or casually. It must be remembered that e-mail is also a means of business correspondence and should be crafted with care.

My thanks to my friend, Mrs Vijaya Kumar who suggested that I write this book. I'm also grateful to Ms Kowsalya, my assistant who has helped in the typing of this book.

Nimmoo Kinger

INTRODUCTION

A letter is 'a conversation by post'. A business letter is a commercial conversation and is extremely important in furthering business relationships. Business transactions now, more than ever, span the globe and it is the business letter which spans the physical distance between business partners. The reputation and prestige of a commercial undertaking depends on the standard of its written communications. The effectiveness of an organization's business letters determines the success or failure of the enterprise.

Functions of a Business Letter

The five reasons for writing business letters are:

1. To provide a convenient and inexpensive means of communication
2. To seek or give information
3. To furnish evidence of transactions
4. To provide a record for future reference
5. To build goodwill

Essentials of a Business Letter

A business letter must be concise, precise and at the same time warm and courteous. The focus must be on the recipient, as a person. The 'You' attitude should be adopted.

For example:

Thank you for your assurance that you have adequate information on the product in order to enable you to place your order with us.

An effective business letter is positive in tone, natural and written in simple language.

Tact and persuasion play an important role. Matters of delay in execution of order, requesting for early payments of bills, refusing credit, etc need to handle with tact. Persuasiveness helps in selling ideas, goods and services. A good business letter is a salesman in print.

A businessman will have many occasions when he has to refuse, disagree, complain. He cannot do this in a forthright manner, however justified he may be in plain speaking. He needs to clothe his communication in a pleasant and positive manner.

For example:

Negative Approach: We regret to inform you that we will not be able to execute your order until your payment is received.

Positive Approach: Thank you for your order. The goods will be sent to you as soon as we receive the payment.

Negative Approach: It is very unfortunate that your payment was received too late to permit us to dispatch your goods.

Positive Approach: It was kind of you to send us a Demand Draft for your order of March 10. However, your goods were mailed C O D last Monday since our credit department assumed that you would want them as quickly as possible.

Make liberal use of the following phrases:

We shall be glad to...
It is a pleasure...
Thank you...
With our compliments...
Your kind letter...
Many thanks for your...
We are pleased to...
We will be glad to...

Language of a Business Letter

The language of a business letter should be natural and as close to spoken English as far as possible. There is no place for the old 'Business English'. The language should be simple and straight forward.

For example:

Formal: 'We acknowledge, with thanks, your letter of 5th July which shall have our prompt attention.'

A more direct and effective approach would be: 'Thank you for your letter of 5th July. It shall receive our prompt attention.'

AVOID THE FOLLOWING

1. Obvious, Trite, Irritating Expressions

- Replying to your letter of......
- This is to inform you...
- We are aware of the contents of your...
- We are glad to invite your kind attention to...
- We are pleased to announce..

- We wish to call your attention to..
- Please be advised that…
- I should like to say that...
- You will be pleased to know...
- ….. and oblige.
- …. Have noted its contents/contents noted.
- Don't pass this up…
- Trusting this will be satisfactory…
- Just sign on the dotted line…
- You will be sorry if you don't order now…

2. Phrases That Have Been Worn Thin From Overuse

- Have you hear about…
- Here it is! The product you have been waiting for
- No doubt you have…

3. Flat, Redundant Phrases

- for your information
- hereby/heretofore/herewith
- I have your letter…
- I wish to thank/may I ask
- our Mr....
- permit me to say
- pursuant to…
- thank you again
- thank you in advance
- thereon….
- as the case may be…
- at hand/on hand....

- the above ....
- your esteemed favour.....
- acknowledge receipt of ......
- duly

REDUNDANT EXPRESSIONS

Don't Use.....	Use....
Above mentioned	referred to above
According to our records	our records show or we find that
Advise, inform	say, tell
Along these lines /on the order of	like, similar to
And et cetera	et cetera
Anticipating your reply	we look forward to your reply
As otherwise	otherwise
As per	according to
As to your suggestion	regarding your suggestion
As a matter of fact	in fact
At about	about
At all times	always
At an early date	soon, today, next week, a specific date
At this time/at the present time	now, at present
At your earliest convenience/at the earliest possible	as soon as possible
Attached hereto	attached

Attached you will find	attached are or we attach
Avail oneself of	use
Awaiting your esteemed	we shall wait for your reply /we wait for your instructions.
Before 12 noon	forenoon
Be of the opinion	believe
Both alike	together
By return mail	at once
Check into	at once
Cheque to cover	cheque for
Come to a decision	decide
Communication	letter
Connect up	connect
Continue up	continue
Cooperate together	cooperate
Costs the sum of	costs
Customary practice	practice
Deem	believe, consider
Each and every	each for every
Enclosed herewith/enclosed please find	enclosed
Enter into	enter
Even date	today
Favour	letter, memo, et al
For a period of a month	for a month
For the purpose of	for
Forward	send
Forward by post	mail
Free of charge	free

Have a tendency to	tend to
I have pleasure to inform (in informing) you	I am pleased to tell you
If you will refer to your file	please refer your file
In a satisfactory manner	satisfactorily
In accordance with	according to
In advance of prior to	before
In compliance with, in accordance with your request	as you requested, as requested by you
In due course/time	soon
In many instances	often
In re, re	regarding, concerning
In the amount of	for
In the course of	during
In the event that/of	if, in case
In the near future	soon
In the amount of	about
In the process of being	being
In this day and age	nowadays
In view of the circumstances	as
Inform of the reason	tell why
Kindly	please
Kindly advise	please let us know
Letter under date of	letter of
Letter with regard to	letter about
New beginner	beginner
Of recent date	recent
On account of the fact that	because
On receipt of	when we receive

On Tuesday next, the 14th instant	next Tuesday
Only too pleased to	very glad to
Owing to the fact that	because
Party	person, a specific name
Past experience	experience
Place emphasis on	emphasise
Place an order for	order
Please be good to inform us	please inform us, please let us know your comments
Please so advise us	please let us know
Purchase	buy
Repeat	repeat
Said	not to be used as an adjective
Same	not to be used as a noun
Same identical	identical
Send an answer	reply
Subsequent to	after, since
Take into consideration	consider
Terminate	end
Thank you, we remain	thank you
The above mentioned merchandise	the merchandise
The party you suggested	the person you suggested
The said shipment	the shipment
The undersigned, the writer	I/me
The writer has investigated	I have investigated
To make an inspection	to see them
Trusting you will send	please send

Under date of 7th December	on 7th December
Under separate cover	separately
Under the circumstances	because
Until such time as	until
Up above	above
Up to this writing	until now
Utilize	use
We acknowledge with thanks your letter of	we thank you for your letter of
We are in receipt of	we have
We are ready this time to	we are writing today
We are writing to tell you	this explains
We beg to acknowledge your letter of	we thank you for your letter of
We beg to state	we would like to say
We beg to thank you for	thank you for
We deem it advisable	it would be better
We extend our apologies	we are sorry/we apologise
We extend our thanks for	thanks for
We shall advise you	we shall let you know
We take pleasure	we are glad
We take this opportunity	we have the pleasure to/ we are pleased to
We wish to thank you	we thank you
We would like to be advised	please let us know
We would recommend	we recommend
We would request that you	please
We would suggest	we suggest

We regard to the estimate required	requesting an estimate
With reference/regard/respect to	about, regarding
Write your name	sign
Your favour of the 9th instant	your letter of 9th may
Your good self	you
You have our permission	you may
Your letter is at hand	we have your letter
Your valued instructions	your instructions

LAYOUT AND FORM OF A BUSINESS LETTER

A **business letter** is more formal than a personal letter. It should have a margin of at least one inch on all four edges. It is always written on 8½"x11' (or metric equivalent) unlined stationery. There are **six** parts to a business letter.

1. **The Heading**

   This contains the return address (usually two or three lines) with the date on the last line.

   Sometimes it may be necessary to include a line after the address and before the date for a phone number, fax number, E-mail address, or something similar.

   Often a line is skipped between the address and date. That should always be done if the heading is next to the left margin.

   It is not necessary to type the return address if you are using stationery with the return address already imprinted. Always include the date.

2. **The Inside Address**

   This is the address you are sending your letter to. Make it as complete as possible. Include titles and names if you know them. This is always on the left margin.

   If an 8½" x 11" paper is folded in thirds to fit in a standard 9" business envelope, the inside address can appear through the window in the envelope.

An inside address also helps the recipient route the letter properly and can help should the envelope be damaged and the address become unreadable.

Skip a line after the heading before the inside address. Skip another line after the inside address before the greeting.

3. **The Greeting**

Also called the salutation. The greeting in a business letter is always formal. It normally begins with the word "Dear" and always includes the person's last name.

It normally has a title. Use a first name only if the title is unclear—for example, you are writing to someone named "Leslie, " but do not know whether the person is male or female.

4. **The Body**

The body is written as text. A business letter is never hand written. Depending on the letter style you choose, paragraphs may be indented. Regardless of format, skip a line between paragraphs.

Skip a line between the greeting and the body. Skip a line between the body and the close.

5. **The Complimentary Close**

This short, polite closing ends with a comma. It is either at the left margin or its left edge is in the centre, depending on the business letter style that you use. It begins at the same column the heading does.

The block style is becoming more widely used because there is no indenting to bother within the whole letter.

6. **The Signature Line**

Skip two lines and type out the name to be signed. This customarily includes a middle initial, but does not have to. Women may indicate how they wish to be addressed by placing **Miss, Mrs., Ms.** or similar title in parentheses before their name.

The signature line may include a second line for a title, if appropriate.

The signature should start directly above the first letter of the signature line in the space between the close and the signature line. Business letters should not contain postscripts.

Elements of a Business Letter

Heading ______________________

____

____

____

Date ______________________

Your Reference ______________________

Our Reference ______________________

____

Inside Address ______________________

____

____

____

Attention ______________________

____

Salutation

Subject

Body

Complimentary Close

Signature

Identification Marks

Enclosure

CONTENTS

1
INQUIRY LETTERS

This section focuses on the inquiry letter. The *inquiry letter* is useful when you need information, advice, names, or directions. Be careful, however, not to ask for too much information or for information that you could easily obtain in some other way, for example, by a quick trip to the library.

Inquiry Letters: Types and Contexts

1. There are two types of inquiry letters: *solicited* and *unsolicited*.
2. You write a solicited letter of inquiry when a business or agency advertises its products or services. For example, if a software manufacturer advertises some new packages it has developed and you can't inspect it locally, write a solicited letter to that manufacturer asking specific questions. If you cannot find any information on a technical subject, an inquiry letter to a company involved in that subject may put you on the right track. In fact, that company may supply much more help than you had expected (provided of course that you write a good inquiry letter).
3. Your letter of inquiry is unsolicited if the recipient has done nothing to prompt your inquiry. For example, if

you read an article by an expert, you may have further questions or want more information. You seek help from these people in a slightly different form of inquiry letter. As the steps and guidelines for both types of inquiry letters show, you must construct the unsolicited type more carefully, because recipients of unsolicited letters of inquiry are not ordinarily prepared to handle such inquiries.

Inquiry Letters: Contents and Organization

1. Early in the letter, identify the purpose — to obtain help or information (if it's a solicited letter, information about an advertised product, service, or program).
2. In an unsolicited letter, identify who you are, what you are working on, and why you need the requested information, and how you found out about the individual. In an unsolicited letter, also identify the source that prompted your inquiry, for example, a magazine advertisement.
3. In the letter, list questions or information needed in a clear, specific, and easy-to-read format. If you have quite a number of questions, consider making a questionnaire and including a stamped, self-addressed envelope.
4. In an unsolicited letter, try to find some way to compensate the recipient for the trouble, for example, by offering to pay copying and mailing costs, to accept a collect call, to acknowledge the recipient in your report, or to send him or her a copy of your report. In a solicited letter, suggest that the recipient send brochures or catalogues.

5. In closing an unsolicited letter, express gratitude for any help that the recipient can provide you, acknowledge the inconvenience of your request, but do not thank the recipient "in advance." In an unsolicited letter, tactfully suggest to the recipient that he will benefit by helping you (for example, through future purchases from the recipient's company).

Enquiry About Blood Glucose Monitoring System

Ms Anita Rao,
1102, Andheri West
Sand Marg,
New Delhi

15 July 2004

Dr. Moti,
Director of the Diabetes Clinic
St. JSS Hospital
Ramanuja Road,
Agrahara, Mysore–570 002.

Dear Dr. Moti,

I am writing you in hopes of finding out more about how the new Glucoscan II blood glucose monitoring system, which a representative at Lifescan informed me that your clinic is currently using.

Originally, I saw Lifescan's advertisement of this new device in the January 2004 issue of *Diabetes Forecast* and became very interested in it. I wrote the company and got much useful information, but was recommended to write several current users of the system as well.

For a technical report that I am writing for a technical writing class at JSS Medical College, I need some help with the following questions:

1. How often does the Glucoscan II need to be calibrated in practical, everyday use conditions?
2. How accurate is the Glucoscan II compared to other similar systems that your patients have used?
3. What problems do your patients experience with this new device?

The Lifescan representative indicated that your clinic is one the leaders in implementing this new technology for diabetics, and therefore I am eager to hear from you. In the report I will acknowledge your contributions, and I will send you a copy of the complete report if you wish.

Thank you for your time, and I hope to hear from you soon.

Yours sincerely,

(Anita Rao)
Student, Medical Technology
JSS Medical College

Enquiry About Hardware Support in Version 5.1 of Linux

Ms Sunitha Mittal,
1120 National Park,
Mumbai.

July 12, 2004

Technical Support,
Aptech Software, Inc.,
4201 M G Road, Site 100,
Bangalore.

Dear Technical Support Department:

I am writing this letter to ask you some technical questions about hardware support in version 5.1 of Linux. I saw Aptech Software's advertisement for version 5.1 of Linux in the August, 2003, issue of *Linux Journal*. I was quite impressed with the capabilities as listed in the advertisement, and I would like to learn some more about the product. Before I make the decision to purchase the software, I need to be certain that it will work properly on my computer.

I have three hardware support questions that I would like you to answer. I have reviewed the technical support information at Aptech Software's home page (http://www.redhat.com/), but I have not been able to find answers to my questions. The three hardware-related questions that I have are as follows:

1. Does the latest release of Aptech Linux support the Diamond Viper 330 PCI video card? This card uses the Riva chipset released by NVIDIA Corporation.
2. If Aptech Linux does not currently have a driver for this card, is there a timetable for when the card will be supported?
3. Is there an online site for the latest list of supported hardware. This would be a great aid to me in the future, as I often upgrade my machine.

I am aware that some of the early versions of Aptech Linux were not able to support some of Diamond Multimedia's products, and I hope that new drivers have been created in this latest software release. If the latest release of Aptech Linux can support my video hardware, I will definitely purchase the product. I feel that the price on the product is exceptional, and the range of features is outstanding.

For your convenience, you can respond to me by e-mail. My e-mail address is Sunitha@msn.com. If you prefer to respond by telephone, you can reach me at (044) 215-2155. I appreciate any assistance that you are able to provide me.

Yours sincerely,

(Sunitha Mittal)

Enquiry About Price & Samples

M/S. AMBIKA GENERAL STORES,
Wholesale General Merchants
Distributors & Retailers
Mumbai

19/07/2004

M/s. Kangaroo Staples Ltd.,
Mumbai.

Dear Sir,

Your firm has been recommended to us by Anitha General Store. I wish to introduce ourselves as general merchants of 5 years standing in the market. We add to plan to our stock your 'Staples Pin' brand products.

We are interested in quality goods. Please quote your best prices and sample of 044 staple pins and staple 065 pins. We need at least 30 Boxes set of staple pins.

We look forward to receiving an early reply from you.

Yours faithfully,
For Ambika General Stores,

Proprietor

Reply to the Above

M/S. KANGAROO STAPLES LTD.,
Mumbai

M/s. Ambika General Stores,
Wholesale General Merchants,
Distributors & Retailers,
Mumbai. 21/07/2004

Dear Sir,

We are very glad to know, from your letter of 19th July that you are interested in stocking our products.

The Kangaroo Staple Pins products are successfully marching ahead in all markets they have entered.

We are pleased to quote you the following prices, common for all Staple.

044 Staples Pins Medium Quality *(a box contain 100 pins)*	Rs. 120.00
044 Staples Pins Best Quality *(a box contain 150 pins)*	Rs. 275.00
065 Staples Pins Medium Quality *(a box contain 100 pins)*	Rs. 250.00
065 Staples Pins Best Quality *(a box contain 150 pins)*	Rs. 350.00

Please note that the trade discount at 10% for an order for 50 box set or more.

We assure you of the dispatch of the consignment within five days of the receipt of your orders.

We are sending a sample of Staple pins. We look forward to serving you.

Yours faithfully,
For Kangaroo Staples Limited

(Subramaniyam S P)
Sales Manager

Enquiry for Catalogue & Price List

Mr. Ram Srivatsav,
Mumbai. 19/07/2004

M/s. Cyber Private Limited,
Dhanvanthi Road,
Mumbai.

Dear Sir,

We have seen your advertisement in *Bombay Express* dt. 19/07/2004 regarding the discount for Printer. Kindly send us your latest illustrated catalogue and price-list of "Sony Printer".

Thank you.

Yours faithfully,

(Ram Srivatsav)

Reply to the Above

CYBER PRIVATE LIMITED,
Dhanvanthi Road,
Mumbai.

Mr. Ram Srivatsav,
Mumbai. 20/07/2004

Dear Sir,

We are sorry that we failed to enclose our catalogue with our letter of the Sony Printer. We will send you our catalogue within 1 or 2 weeks.

Thank you.

Yours faithfully,
For Cyber Private Limited

Manager

Reply to Enquiry for Spare Parts

KIRAN CORPORATION
Mysore

M/s. Star Garage,
Mangalore. 20/07/2004

Dear Sir,

We thank you for your enquiry for the Spare Parts. We can supply immediately through Patel Roadways by 21/07/2004 at Rs.50 per Set of Spanner, Rs.150 per Jumper.

Thank you.

Yours faithfully,
For Kiran Corporation

Manager

Reply to the Above

CYBER PRIVATE LIMITED
Dhanvanthi Road,
Mumbai.

Mr. Ram Srivatsav,
Mumbai. 20/07/2004

Dear Sir,

We have received your various letters with regards "Sony Printer" and must apologize for the long delay in dealing with this matter, which is not an easy one. We hope to be able to give you a definite answer soon.

Thank you.

Yours faithfully,
For Cyber Private Limited

Manager

Apology Letter

CYBER PRIVATE LIMITED
Dhanvanthi Road,
Mumbai.

Mr. Ram Srivatsav,
Mumbai. 20/07/2004

Dear Sir,

We must apologize for not having replied before to your letter on the above, but regret that the matter is still in abeyance. As soon as it has been brought to a satisfactory conclusion, we shall write to you again.

Thank you.

Yours faithfully,
For Cyber Private Limited

Manager

Reply to Enquiry for Printer

CYBER PRIVATE LIMITED
Dhanvanthi Road,
Mumbai.

20/07/2004

Dear Mr. Ram Srivatsav,

We thank you for your enquiry of 19th July and we glad to know that you are impressed by our advertisement in "Bombay Express".

The enclosed catalogue will give you all necessary details about our printers. The price quoted by us are very competitive. In view of the large business promised, you will be given a special trade discount of 20% on "Dot Matrix Sony Printer" and "Laser Sony Printer" at 15%.

	Price	**Discount**
Dot Matrix Sony Printer	Rs. 45, 000/-	20%
Laser Sony Printer	Rs. 65, 000/-	15%

We assure you of our immediate attention to your orders.

Yours faithfully,
For Cyber Private Limited,

Sales Manager

Enquiry for Price of Book

REGIONAL EDUCATION TRUST
Manasagangothri,
Mysore.

M/s. Saraswathi Book House,
KRS Circle,
Mysore. 19/07/2004

Dear Sir,

We have seen your stand at the Book Fair in Jaganmohan Palace Hall. We are interested in placing an order for 50 copies of Kuvempu's Ramayanadarshanam, 2004 edition. Please quote price list and the date of releasing of the book.

Thanking you.

Yours faithfully,
For Regional Education Trust

(M N Ramachandra)

Reply to the Above

M/s. SARASWATHI BOOK HOUSE
KRS Circle,
Mysore.

19/07/2004

Regional Education Trust,
Manasagangothri,
Mysore.

Dear Sir,

Thank you for your letter 19th July 2004. The new edition of Kuvempu's Sri Ramayanadharshnam will be released on 25th of this month and the price of the book is Rs. 250/-. Since you wish to place an order for 50 copies, the books will be sent to you free of transportation and packing charges.

We hope to receive your confirmed order soon.

Thank you.

Yours faithfully,
For Saraswathi Book House,

(H N Gowda)
Proprietor

Request for Price List

M/s. RAM LAL TRADERS
Wholesale dealer,
Mannas Market,
Mysore.

19/07/2004

M/s. Uncle Chips Pvt. Ltd.,
Srirangapatanam.

Dear Sir,

We have an enquiry for large quantities of Chips. We request you to quote the price of your varieties of chips. Please send the sample as early as possible so that we may be able to place our order soon. We hope you will quote the lowest possible price.

Awaiting your reply.

Thank you.

Yours faithfully,
For Ram Lal Traders

(Bharat Lal)
Partner

Reply to the Above

M/s. UNCLE CHIPS PVT. LTD.,
Srirangapatanam.

19/07/2004

M/s. Ram Lal Traders,
Wholesale dealer,
Mannas Market,
Mysore.

Dear Sir,

Thank you for your letter of 19th July 2004. We are sending you samples of our new products along with a price list of all the varieties of chips available with us. These chips are very reasonably priced and can be sent you at one week's notice.

Thank you.

Yours faithfully,
For Uncle Chips Pvt. Ltd.,

(Shankar Pillai)
Marketing Executive

Price List for Horlicks

M/s. HOME NEEDS,
Mumbai.

M/s. Mohan Bhandar,
Mysore.

19/07/2004

Dear Sir,

In response to your enquiry dated 10th July 2004, we are pleased to quote our price for "Horlicks". Our price for the case (contains 20 bottles of 500 grams of Horlicks) is Rs. 1750/- plus taxes at actuals.

Transportation charges from Mumbai to Mysore will be Rs. 175/- on VRL Transport.

Awaiting your reply.

Thank you.

Yours faithfully,

(G R Radhakrishnan)
Proprietor

Enquiry for Price List

Mr. S Gururaj,
M/s. Mysore Tarpaulins,
Mysore.

20/07/2004

M/s. Weather Maker,
Mumbai.

Attn.: **Ms. Usha Bhargav**–*Sales Manager*

Dear Madam,

Sub: **Enquiry for Inrubber Products**

With reference to your offer of Inrubber Products dated 25/04/2004 we should be glad if you could let us have samples in the following sizes/colors/quantities.

Please quote your best price, for 500 units of each of three items viz, Light-weight Overcoats, Weatherproof Raincoats and Easywear Gumboots in medium and small sizes (all equal number) and for both men and women. Let us know whether you can dispatch the goods within 15 days of the receipt of the order. We would also like to negotiate terms for larger orders.

We look forward to receiving any early reply from you.

Thank you.

Yours faithfully,
For Mysore Tarpaulins

(S Gururaj)
Proprietor

Reply to the Above

M/s. WEATHER MAKER
Mumbai.

M/s. Mysore Tarpaulins,
Mysore. 20/07/2004

Dear Mr. Gururaj,

Thank you for you letter dt. 20/07/2004. In reply to your enquiry for Inrubber Products we should be glad if you could call at our office on the 23rd of this month at 5.30 p.m. Our Sales Manager is on a Southern region tour and will back on 22nd of this month.

Thank you.

Yours faithfully,
For Weather Maker

Authorized Signatory

Reply for Enquiry for Catalogue

SHENGAN MACHINERY & ELECTRICAL
EQUIPMENT DEVELOPMENT COMPANY
Beijing.

A P Electrical Enterprises,
Mumbai.

3rd May 2004

Dear Sirs,

We are glad to know you are interested in our aluminum composite panel (ACP, widely used in interior/exterior wall) production lines. We are the sole exporter for full set of ACP production lines in China, and up to now, we have successfully provided our clients world wide with over 75 ACP production lines as well as many of other kinds of ACP (PVDF/Polyester paint). The products have very good features and are reasonably priced.

Our catalogue is enclosed for your reference.

We can provide you with the best services wherever you are in the world! We look forward to hearing from you very soon.

Yours faithfully,
For Shengan Machinery & Electrical Equipment Development Company

(S Lee)
Manager

2
QUOTATIONS LETTERS

A quotation is a specific offer for sale. It is made in response to an enquiry from a particular person or business house. A quotation includes details about the prices of the specific goods desired, terms of payment, condition of delivery and other details.

Quotation for Furniture

DURGA ENTERPRISES
No. 47, Surya Bakery,
Hebbal – 7, Mysore.

22/08/2004

M/s. Nakshatra Furnitures,
Malabar,
Mumbai.

Dear Sirs,

We intend to buy the following items of furniture for our new branch to be opened shortly in Subhash Market, Janakpuri. Please quote your lowest rates and also indicate the terms and conditions of payment.

Qty	Item	Specifications
35	Single pedestal steel Grey-coloured desks	Length 60" Width 40" Height 28"
6	Double pedestal steel Grey-coloured desks	Length 62" Width 48" Height 28"
8	Typist's posture steel chairs with seats and backrests padded with foam	Height 16" (adjustable upto 20") Width 17" Length 12" (from back to front) Depth of backrest 5" Width of backrest 10" Colour: Sky blue

We look forward to hearing from you soon.

Yours faithfully,

(R.T. Mahesh)
Purchase Officer

Reply to the Above

NAKSHATRA FURNITURES
Malabar, Mumbai-7.

Tele No. 5142 0000
Fax No. 5142 3330

M/s. Durga Enterprises,
Mysore.

Dear Sir,

Many thanks for your letter No. SAM/DC02/04-05 dated. 22/04/2004.

We are pleased to quote the following rates for the furniture you require.

	Item Description	Nett Price Each
1.	Single pedestal steel gre-coloured desks (60" x 40" x 28")	Rs. 1425.00
2.	Double pedestal steel grey-coloured desks (62" x 48" x 28")	Rs. 1963.50
3.	Typist's posture steel chairs with seat and backrest padded with foam (height adjustable from 16" to 20"; width 17", length 12" (from back to from); depth of backrest 5", width of backrest 10", colour sky blue) Sales Tax @ 7 ½ %	Rs. 846.50

Packing and transportation charges from our works to Subhash Market and other duties and taxes are included in the price quoted above.

We hope to receive your order soon and help you to furnish your new branch office without delay. We assure you of our prompt services and shall deliver the goods within a fortnight of the receipt of your order.

A folder describing the KASTWKK furniture we manufacture is enclosed to make it convenient for you to select any other items you may wish to buy now or in future.

Yours faithfully,

(Hari Prasad)
Manager

Quotation for Garments

LAKME GARMENTS INDIA (P) LTD.
Mumbai.

M/s. Queen Fashion House,
Mumbai.

20/07/2004

Dear Ms. Mathur,

With reference to your telephone enquiry of this afternoon we can offer you the following at the prices stated: for 100 Meters.

1. Lace Cloth Material at Rs. 17, 500/-
2. Plain Material at Rs. 25, 250/-
3. Machine Embroidery Material at Rs. 52, 275/-.

Transportation charges, taxes and other duties included in the price quoted above. We hope to receive your order soon.

Thank you.

Yours faithfully,
For Lakme Garments India Private Limited,

Managing Director

Offer of Vegetables

THE GARDEN PRODUCE SUPPLY CO.
6, Convent Garden, Nainital.

20th January 2004

Mr. S. K. Kataria,
M/s. Udai Vegetable Mart,
Greengrocer,
Darjeeling.

Dear Sir,

Having bought large stocks of peas and beans, we are pleased to offer you ex-warehouse here, and for delivery until February, as follows:

Large Peas	Rs. 15, 750/- Per Tonne
Small Peas	Rs. 17, 750/- Per Tonne
Green Beans	Rs. 7, 250/- Per cwt
White Beans	Rs. 6, 751/- Per cwt

The minimum quantity for peas is one tonne, and for beans half a quintal.

We shall be glad to make you special offers for orders of not less than a truck load at a time.

Yours faithfully,
For The Garden Produce Supply Co.

Partner

Reply to the Above

UDAI VEGETABLE MART
Greengrocer, Darjeeling.

Mr. Ashuthosh Rana,
M/s. The Garden Produce Supply Co.,
6, Convent Garden,
Nainital.

27th January 2004

Dear Sir,

In reply to your circular of 20th January, I am willing to purchase 2 tonnes of Large Peas if you can reduce the price to Rs. 2145/- per tonne against cash.

We look forward for your early reply.

Yours faithfully,
For Udai Vegetable Mart

(S. K. Kataria)
Proprietor

Reply to the Above

THE GARDEN PRODUCE SUPPLY CO.,
6, Convent Garden, Nainital.

05th February 2004

Mr. S. K. Kataria,
M/s. Udai Vegetable Mart,
Greengrocer,
Darjeeling.

Dear Sir,

In reply to your letter of the 27th January, we regret that it is impossible for us to supply you with Large Peas in the quality of the Sample quoted at Rs. 2145/- per tonne.

However, in order to meet you, we are prepared to reduced the price to Rs. 1150/- against cash, a quotation from which we cannot budge.

We hope that you will soon place your order, and assure you of its most careful execution.

Yours faithfully,
For The Garden Produce Supply Co.

Partner

Catalogue and Quotation Forwarded

SHARIFF FURNITURES
Station Road, Chennai.

Mr. G.P. Chengappa,
Main Road,
Tirupathi.

12th November 2003

Dear Sir,

We thank you for your letter of 8th November, and are sending you by this post catalogue containing quotations for large orders taken from our existing stock. You will also find the times of delivery and the terms of payment indicated there. Export packing will be charge at the lowest possible process, but there is no charge for the packing of the separate articles.

We recommend the catalogue to your careful perusal and wait for your orders.

Yours faithfully,
For Shariff Furnitures

(Irfan Pattan)
Manager

Quotations for Shoes

LALBAGH SHOE MANUFACTURING CO.,
Agra.

M/s. Clean Shoe Suppliers Ltd.,
Connaught Place,
New Delhi.

5th November 2004

Sir,

We thank you for the enquiry made and accordingly we are furnishing below the prices of shoes.

Cock-plume shoe	Rs. 335/- per pair
Peacock-plume shoe	Rs. 465/- per pair
Pea-hen plume shoe	Rs. 523/- per pair

We shall allow a special trade discount of 10% on all purchases. This offer will remain open for a fortnight from the date of receipt of this letter.

We hope you will place your order with us.

Yours faithfully,
For Lalbagh Shoe Manufacturing Co.

Asst. Manager

Quotations for Pumping Machines

EMPSON PUMPING STORE
D.D. Urs Road, Mysore.

M/s. Thompson & Jones,
Mumbai.

5th May 2004

Dear Sir,

Thank you for your letter of the 3rd May, informing me that you want to place your order for three pumping machines with me. I can deliver by the 1st August, although the term is very short.

I should be able to supply the three pumping machines as per drawings send as follows:

No. 1 at Rs. 15, 750/-

No. 2 at Rs. 20, 745/-

No. 3 at Rs. 21, 750/-

Ex works, Mumbai, net cash against three months acceptance.

I have quoted you so low that another firm will scarcely be in position to make you a more favourable bid, and deliver faultless workmanship. I trust, therefore, you will place the order, and, as the time is short, send your reply immediately.

Yours faithfully,
For Empson Pumping Store

Manager

Inviting Quotation for Tiles

Mr. D N Thimmayya,
1, Pickle Street,
Mangalore.

1st January 2004

M/s. Glorious Tiles Ltd.,
10, Connaught Circus,
New Delhi.

Dear Sir,

Please send us your quotations for the following varieties of tiles specially manufactured by your company at Bangalore.

1.	Red Tiles	: 10" x 10" per thousand
2.	Green Tiles	: 12" x 12" per thousand
3.	Black and White Tiles	: 10" x 10" per thousand
4.	Glorious Special Tiles	: 20" x 20" per thousand

Also please inform that what discount is permissible on these tiles.

We would appreciate a prompt response.

Yours faithfully,

(D N Thimmayya)

Reply to the Above

GLORIOUS TILES LTD.,
10, Connaught Circus, New Delhi.

Mr. D N Thimmayya,
1, Pickle Street,
Mangalore.

10th January 2004

Dear Sir,

Thank you very much for your enquiry dated January 1 2004. We wish to quote the following prices for bulk supply of more than 1, 000 tiles (each variety) from our Bangalore unit.

1.	Red Tiles	10" x 10" per thousand	Rs.5500/-
2.	Green Tiles	12" x 12" per thousand	Rs.7300/-
3.	Black and White Tiles	10" x 10" per thousand	Rs.5025/-
4.	Glorious Special Tiles	20" x 20" per thousand	Rs.6090/-

You will appreciate that this is a very low price which is offered because of the size of your order and the confidence we have that we shall do further business together.

Assuring you of our personal attention at all times.

Yours faithfully,
For Glorious Tiles Ltd.,

Manager

Inviting Quotations for Car Accessories

KHANNA BROTHERS LIMITED,
42, M.M. Road, Trombay.

PL/FT
M/s. Car Accessories Ltd.,
Poona.

July 30, 2004

Dear Sirs,

We would appreciate further information with regard to the Radiator Muffs and Radiator Blinds advertised by you in the current issue of your catalogue.

We hope to be able to order large quantities of these and trust that you can offer us a really competitive quotation.

Yours faithfully,
For Khanna Brothers Limited.

Asst. Manager

Reply to the Above

M/S. CAR ACCESSORIES LTD.,
Poona.

Your Ref: PL/FT
Our Ref: DG/RT/156

M/s. Khanna Brothers Limited,
42, M.M. Road,
Trombay.

17th July 2004

Dear Sirs,

We thank you for your enquiry of the 2nd December concerning our Radiator Muffs and Radiator Blinds. We are pleased to say that we are prepared to reduce our catalogue prices by 6 per cent if your total order for this season amount to 1, 000 of these items. This is the lowest offer we can make and I hope that you will agree that it compares favourably with the prices quoted by our competitors.

Our terms of payment are set out in the catalogue.

Yours faithfully,
For Car Accessories Ltd.,

Manager

Asking Estimate for Printing Job

RAMESH PUBLISHING HOUSE,
Daryaganj, New Delhi.

M/s. Seema Printers,
Delhi–110006.

20th August 2004

Dear Sirs,

We shall be glad to have your estimates for the printing of a book as per details below:

Size	: (20 x 30)/16
Quantity	: 15, 000
No. of Forms	: 40 (approx.)
Paper	: will be supplied by us
Type	: 10 pt. Universe; underlined matter bold-italics, heading–14 pt. Bold caps and 12 pt. Bold.
Chapters	: Each chapter to start from a new page
Spacing	: Single except with new paras where it should be double

Neatly typed manuscript in double space is ready with us.

An immediate response will be highly appreciated.

Yours faithfully,
For Ramesh Publishing House,

Editor

Sending Estimates

SEEMA PRINTERS
Delhi–6.

M/s. Ramesh Publishing House,
Daryaganj,
New Delhi.

23rd June 2004

Dear Sirs,

We thank you for your enquiry of 20th August and have pleasure in submitting our estimates as under:

Rates	Rs. 300 per form per thousand
Time	2 months from the date of collecting MSS.
Payment	Cash/Cheque

These estimates are the most competitive and we are sure that will meet your requirements.

Assuring you of our best services, and full cooperation always.

Yours faithfully,
For Seema Printers

Manager

Public Tender

Sealed tenders are invited by State Trading Corporation of India for the following items which are lying in Godown No. 5, Juhu Road, Mumbai.

S.N.	Items
1.	2 Ambassdor Cars 1988-A-One condition, mileage 64, 000 k.m.
2.	A Voltas Air Conditioner – 2 tonne, partly bent on left hand top in perfect running condition.
3.	Bajaj Chetak 1981-Mileage 20, 000 k.m- front type slightly damaged-no stepney.
4.	Polar Fan – 45".

Tender forms may be collected from the office of the STC between 4 to 5.30 p.m. on any working day.

Separate tender form for each item together with cash Rs. 5000/-, each for the first three items and Rs. 800/- for fans should be submitted before the closing hours of the office on 20th October.

Tenders will be opened in presence of the public on the same day at 1 p.m.

Goods will have to be removed from our godown before 5 p.m. on the same day after paying the balance money in cash or by bank draft. Cheques will not be accepted.

Payment will be refunded for unaccepted tenders on 21st and 22nd October between 10 a.m. to 12 noon.

Sd/

Manager (Stores)

3
ORDER LETTERS

If the quotation is found satisfactory, the buyer accepts it and drafts a letter or sends printed form stating therein the quantity, unit price and the amount of the goods. This is known as order.

Full and correct particular of their quality, size, colour, indicate the type of packing, mention the price and terms of which the goods are being ordered, indicate clearly the address to which goods are to be delivered, give special instruction for packing, insurance, payment of customs duty; mention the mode of transport.

The cancellation of an order by the buyer is done due to inordinate delay in the execution of order; fall in the market price or bankruptcy of the customer.

Order for Suitcase

DAGAR ENTERPRISES
472 A, New Rohtak Road, Bhiwani 125021.

12 October 2004

Kashiwal Plastic Limited,
234, Subhash Shinde Road,
Churchgate,
Bombay - 400 029.

Subject: **Order for Supply of Karywel Suitcases**

Dear Sirs,

One of our business contacts in Delhi has informed us that the Karywel suitcases manufactured by you are light, durable, soft-coloured and well-designed and that their sale is picking up fast. This information has aroused our interest in your product.

We have been selling portmanteaus, canvas bags and plastic purses for the last 25 years and our average annual turnover is about Rs. 6 lakhs. Now we wish to add to the rank of our merchandise.

A recent consumer survey in Bhiwani has revealed that there is a market for the kind of suitcase you manufacture. Our estimated quarterly requirement is as follows:

Type	Size	Quantity
Karywel picnic	18"	75
Karywel feather	20"	40
Karywel tourist	22"	50
Karywel wedding	24"	35
		200

To begin with, please supply 200 suitcases as per details give above on 30-days credit terms. We would also like to have similar terms for future purchases.

To help you make a decision, I am listing as references the names of our bank and a manufacturer from whom we have been purchasing goods for the last ten years on credit basis.

[i] State Bank of India
Mandir Chowk,
Station Road,
Bhiwani - 125 020.

[ii] Beniwal Canvas Works
Dharmatalla,
Trigun Sen Road,
Calcutta - 600 036.

If you need any further information, we shall be glad to furnish it.

Yours faithfully,

(Ram Das)
Manager

Positive Reply to the Above

KASHIWAL PLASTICS LIMITED
234, Subhash Shinde Road,
Churchgate
Mumbai-400 029

10 November 2003

The Manager,
Dagar Enterprises,
472A, New Rohtak road,
Bhiwani - 125 021.

Subject: **Supply of Karywel Suitcases**

Dear Sir,

Please refer to your letter dated 12 October, 2004 We are please to accept you as a credit customer of our company. Your order for 200 suitcases is being sent immediately through Golden Transport Company on the credit terms proposed by you. A bill for Rs. 55, 000/- is enclosed. You will notice that we have allowed the usual trade discount, and that the later date by which the payment should reach us is 9 January 2004.

The shipping papers have been sent separately to your bank.

We have investigated the credit references given by you and found them satisfactory. We look forward to serving you in future and hope to receive an order for another lot soon. We wish you success in promoting the sale of Karywel.

A form for credit information is sent herewith in duplicate. Please fill it in and send us one copy. This request is a part of our credit procedure and helps us update our records as regards our credit customers.

Yours faithfully,

(P.K. Saxena)
Credit Manager

Negative Reply to Above

KASHIWAL PLASTICS LIMITED
234, Subhash Shinde Road,
Churchgate, Bombay-400 029

10 November 2003

The Manager,
Dagar Enterprises,
472A, New Rohtak Road,
Bhiwani - 125 021.

Subject: **Supply of Karywel Suitcases**

Dear Sir,

We appreciate your interest in our products and than you for your order dated 12 October 2003 for the supply of 200 Karywel suitcases on credit basis.

We have gathered the relevant information about your financial standing. Unfortunately is not in keeping with our customary requirement for establishing credit arrangement with a buyer.

However, if the situation changes, we would be pleased to grant you that desired credit privileges. In the meantime we would be glad to supply your order on receipt of a demand draft for Rs. 55, 000/- as per details given in the enclosed advance invoice. An additional cash discount of 3% is paid by us if the order is accompanied by full payment.

We look forward to hearing from you soon.

Yours faithfully,

(R.K. Saxena)
Credit Manager

Asking Order for Advertised Goods

NEW WELL DONE FURNISHURES
(Furniture Manufacturers)
428, Opp. Hima Canteen,
Hebbal Industrial Area,
Hebbal, Mysore.

Telephone: 251 51 97
Fax: 251 51 98

Your ref: MO/AA *Our ref: PT/RO*

Mr M. Muralidharan Pillai,
Furniture Unit,
Neel Kamal Funiture House,
15, Andri West,
MUMBAI.

15 September 2004

Dear Mr Pillai,

We were very pleased to receive your letter in answer to our advertisement for sofas and armchairs and, as requested, enclose a copy of our latest catalogue. A set of sample materials is being sent under separate cover.

You may be particularly interested in our latest "Today" range which is proving very popular with our customers. The sofa is easily converted into a comfortable double-bed and the armchairs are supplied with matching cushions. You will find particulars of our terms in the price-list printed in the catalogue.

We very much look forward to a trial order. It will enable you to see for yourself the high quality of the material and finish.

Thank you.

Yours sincerely,

(Sadashivaiah Panchaksh)
Managing Director

Encl.: 1 Catalogue

Apologies for Unexpected Delay

MIHEER EXPORT PRIVATE LIMITED
Sector 45/15, Industrial Area,
Mumbai.

Tele: 412 025541
Fax: 412 512562
e-mail: Miheer@Export.com

15/04/2004

M/s. Morico Fashion House,
Bordeaux,
Len Sen,
France.

Dear Sir,

Thank you for your order. At this time we cannot fill your order due to an unexpected shipment delay from our overseas suppliers.

We will hold your order for arrival of the merchandise, and ship shortly thereafter. Unfortunately, we cannot provide you with a specific shipping date at this time.

Thank you for your anticipated patience in this matter.

Yours faithfully,
For Miheer Export Private Limited,

(P.K. Mehtha)
Export Executive.

Apologies for Unexpected Delay

MIHEER EXPORT PRIVATE LIMITED
Sector 45/15, Industrial Area, Mumbai.

Tele: 412 025541
Fax: 412 512562
e-mail: miheer@export.com

M/s. Morio Glass House, 23/07/2004
Nice,
Len Sen, France.

Dear Sir,

This is to inform you that we are unable to make delivery on the above referenced purchase order on the date indicated.

We should have our merchandise ready to ship within 10 days of the original delivery date and we hope that you can hold off until that time.

We did want to inform you of this delay as soon we were advised in order to give you as much time as possible to make alternate arrangements, if necessary. We can assure you, however, that if your order remains in force we will expedite delivery to you as soon as we have received the merchandise.

Please accept our apology for this delay and thank you for your understanding.

Yours faithfully,

(Mahesh Takkar)
Sales Manager

Apology for Delay in Delivering Goods

KIRAN GLASS WARES
No. 22, Mannar's Market,
Mysore-7.

M/s. Pushkaani Glass House,
No. 2, 8th Cross,
Kumaratunga Road,
Colombo.

27/06/2004

Dear Sir,

This is to inform you that we are unable to make delivery on the above referenced purchase order on the date indicated.

We should have our merchandise ready to ship within 10 days of the original delivery date and we hope that you can hold off until that time.

We did want to inform you of this delay as soon we were advised in order to give you as much time as possible to make alternate arrangements, if necessary. We can assure you, however, that if your order remains in force we will expedite delivery to you as soon as we have received the merchandise.

Please accept our apology for this delay and thank you for your understanding.

Thank you.

Yours faithfully,
For Kiran Glass Wares

(Kiran Virani)
Marketing Manager

Packing & Transport

T.K. GHOSH & COMPANY
Sikkim.

30 January 2004

M/s. Sushil Bros & Co.,
Parade Road,
Assam.

Dear Sirs,

We have received your letter of 5th January. We thank you for your order for 100 cases of glassware.

All the containers are clearly marked with the accepted international sign-fragile-top-bottom.

Yours faithfully,

(Lokesh Panchaksh)
Manager

Despatch Details

JYOTI TRADING CO.,
Church Road, Chennai.

M/s. Haripriya Sugandh Co.,
No.5, 7th Cross, 8th Main,
Kuvempunagar,
Mysore - 12.

12 August 2004

Dear Sirs,

Following your letter of 8th August, please find enclosed the details concerning the shipment of our order No A/175.

Each article must be packed in special cases to avoid all risk of damage during transport.

Please deliver the goods to our shipper's warehouse and send the invoice in duplicate.

Yours faithfully,

(Jayanth Balaiah)

4
COMPLAINT AND ADJUSTMENT LETTERS

This section covers two closely related types of business letters: *complaint letters,* which request compensation for problems with purchases or services, and *adjustment letters,* which are the responses to complaint letters.

Complaint Letters

A complaint letter requests some sort of compensation for defective or damaged merchandise or for inadequate or delayed services. While many complaints can be made in person, some circumstances require formal business letters. The complaint may be so complex that a phone call may not effectively resolve the problem; or the writer may prefer the permanence, formality, and seriousness of a business letter. The essential rule in writing a complaint letter is to maintain your poise and diplomacy, no matter how justified your gripe is. Avoid making the recipient an adversary.

Points to Remember

➲ In the letter, identify early the reason you are writing — to register a complaint and to ask for some kind of compensation. Avoid leaping into the details of the problem in the first sentence.

- State exactly what compensation you desire, either before or after the discussion of the problem or the reasons for granting the compensation. (It may be more tactful and less antagonizing to delay this statement in some cases).
- Provide a fully detailed narrative or description of the problem. This is the "evidence."
- Explain why your request should be granted. Presenting the evidence is not enough: state the reasons why this evidence indicates your request should be granted.
- Suggest why it is in the recipient's best interest to grant your request: appeal to the recipient's sense of fairness, desire for continued business, but don't threaten. Find some way to view the problem as an honest mistake. Don't imply that the recipient deliberately committed the error or that the company has no concern for the customer. Toward the end of the letter, express confidence that the recipient will grant your request.

Adjustment Letters

Replies to complaint letters, often called letters of "adjustment, " must be handled carefully when the requested compensation cannot be granted. Refusal of compensation tests your diplomacy and tact as a writer. Here are some suggestions that may help you write either type of adjustment letter:

1. Begin with a reference to the date of the original letter of complaint and to the purpose of your letter. If you deny the request, don't state the refusal right away unless you can do so tactfully.

2. Express your concern over the writer's troubles and your appreciation that he has written you.
3. If you deny the request, explain the reasons why the request cannot be granted in as cordial and non-combative manner as possible. If you grant the request, don't sound as if you are doing so in a begrudging way.
4. If you deny the request, try to offer some partial or substitute compensation or offer some friendly advice (to take the sting out of the denial).
5. Conclude the letter cordially, perhaps expressing confidence that you and the writer will continue doing business.

Delay in Granting Rebate

Mr Prathap Mehra,
No.123, 11th Cross,
Gokulam III Stage,
Mysore – 570 002.

February 12, 2004

M/s Digitech Computer Systems,
P.O. Box 3919,
Mysore – 570 001.

Dear Sir,

This letter is in reference to my purchase of a Magnon JX-200 inkjet printer from Best Price #104 in Mysore on November 11, 2003. Specifically, I am writing about your company's rejection of my request for a rebate as advertised for JX-200 printer.

I originally paid Rs. 15,275 (excluding tax) for the Magnon JX-200 inkjet printer and have since been waiting for the promised Rs. 750 Magnon rebate which was advertised by your company. I just received your letter and was surprised to find you had rejected my rebate claim. I believed I had made it clear as to the reason why I could not provide you with all of the material requested on the rebate coupon, particularly the serial number label from the shipping box, in the original letter (January 15) I sent you with the claim.

Once again, let me emphasize that there were no coupons available at the time when I purchased the BJ-200. Even after repeated visits to Best Price, I did not receive coupons until three weeks later. Unfortunately I had already disposed of the shipping box and consequently the serial number label attached to it and was unable to provide it as requested by the rebate instructions.

This was the reason that I sent a photocopy of the purchase receipt in the original letter even though it was not required. I am now including the original letter with the photocopy of the purchase receipt and a photocopy of the serial number located at the rear of the printer.

Although I am quite happy with the printer, I am very concerned about the problems I am having with this rebate. Especially disturbing is the fact that you stamped MUST BE RESUBMITTED AND POSTMARKED BY JANUARY 31, 2004 on the letter you sent me while the envelope (photocopy included) clearly shows that it was not mailed until February 4, 2004.

In the interest of fair play and in keeping a future customer satisfied, I hope there will be no further delays in resolving this problem. I expect to receive the rebate within the month and thank you for your prompt attention to this matter.

Yours sincerely,

(Prathap Mehra)

Encl.: Copies of original letter, sales receipt, serial number.

Replacement of Faulty Refrigerator

Mr Pramod Malhotra,
1313 Race Course Road,
Bangalore 560 001.

6 June, 2004

Customer Relations/Claims Dept.,
N R R & Sons,
Lakshmi Puram,
Mysore- 570 003.

Dear Sir,

I am writing in regards to a Whirlpool refrigerator that I recently purchased from your company. Because the refrigerator is noisy and is working intermittently. I am requesting repairs, another refrigerator, or a refund equal to the purchase price.

I purchased the refrigerator for Rs. 15, 000/-. The meter was delivered on August 23rd. I also purchased a V-Guard UPS.

Your prompt attention and response would be greatly appreciated as I am put to great inconvenience without a working refrigerator.

Yours sincerely,

(Pramod Malhotra)

Encl.: Purchase Receipt & Xerox copy of Invoice.

Complaint About Defective Sprayers

Mr. J. Ratan Mistra,
774, 4th Cross, 9th Main,
Bannerghata Road,
Bangalore – 560 056.

04 September 2004

Mr. Ram Lal Joshi,
Ram Lal High-Mart Stores,
2400 Highway Road P.O. Box 95,
Bangalore – 560 002.

Dear Mr. Joshi,

I am writing you concerning three polymer lawn and garden sprayers that I have purchased within the last two months from the High-Mart Store in Bangalore. The polymer sprayers are XXL Spray-Master two-gallon hand held sprayers, model number 1992, and cost Rs. 1200.00 each. I purchased the first sprayer on June 28, 2004.

All three of these sprayers had a faulty flow control. The handle control that regulates the amount of spray by the amount of pressure applied in the handle is made of plastic. After about two hours of use, the plastic lever controls wear out. I have followed the instructions that came with the merchandise. All three sprayers have had the same problem. I have exchange the first two sprayers a week after each sale. The third one I have on hand. I have a copy of the receipt and the instructions/parts manual enclosed.

Since this is the only type of sprayer High-Mart stocks and since High-Mart is the only store in Bangalore that carries sprayers, your customers are forced to either buy this faulty sprayer, or go out of town to meet their needs. I am requesting you to either, ask the manufacturer to correct this problem or that you stock a different name brand sprayer. I am also requesting a refund of Rs. 1200/- and information from you indicating progress on this problem.

I choose to do my business in Bangalore and to back High-Mart's belief in buying products from Indian manufacturers to help the local and national economy. Stocking below-standard Indian products forces customers to seek other sources of merchandise, which foreign markets and out of town businesses are only eager to provide.

Yours sincerely,

(J. Ratan Mistra)

Encl.: Copy of receipt and invoice.

Compensation for Poor Quality of Cosmetics

Ms Naina Gupta,
P.O. Box 2572,
Chennai.

November 19, 2004

Ms. Kavitha Ramaswamy,
Manager,
Chitra Cosmetics,
1001 Airport Blvd,
Chennai.

Dear Ms. Kavitha,

Sincerely, I am writing you concerning a problem that has arisen from the purchase of one of your cosmetic products on August 16, 2004 at the Alankar's Mainland Mall Store. The item is your Chitra Ultra Sable Mascara priced at Rs. 750.95. The sales girl sold me this mascara, two shades of blush and a jar of cold cream on this date.

The problem developed shortly after applying this mascara for the first time. Within one hour, my eyelids became puffy and red and began to itch. After two hours, my entire eye area was swollen and remained so for two days. No other cosmetic product had been applied to my eye area, and I feel sure that this mascara caused an allergic reaction. I have used various brands of mascara including Estee Lauder, Channel and Maybeline and have never experienced this sort of reaction before. My dermatologist advised not to use your Chitra product again. I also incurred a dermatologist fee of Rs. 150.00. Copies of receipts for these services and the mascara purchase are included in this letter.

I would appreciate being compensated for to the extent of Rs. 850.95 to reimburse me for the doctor's visit, and for the purchase price of the mascara.

I have used many of your products in the past without any problems and hope to continue a positive relationship with your company and its products in the future.

Thank you.

Yours sincerely,

(Naina Gupta)

Encl.: 2 Bills.

Adjustment for Damaged Freight

M/s. ROSEMOUNT CORPORATION
117, Jayanagara
Bangalore.

July 14, 2004

Mrs. Pramila Sharma,
Complete Table, Inc.,
P.O. Box 3132,
Mysore.

Sub.: **Your letter of March 24 about damaged freight**

Dear Mrs. Sharma,

I have just received your March 24 letter about the damaged shipment you received through Rosemount Corporation Freight and regret the inconvenience that it has caused you.

From your account of the problem, I am quite sure that your request for the Rs. 550 adjustment on the damage to the 2 crates of Tea powder will be granted. A certain amount of breakage of this sort does unavoidably occur in cross-country shipping; I am sorry that it was your company that had to be the one to suffer the delay.

I must remind you to keep the damaged crates in the same condition in which you received them until one of our representatives can inspect them. That inspection should take place within 2 weeks.

If all is in order, as it sounds to be in your letter, you can expect the full reimbursement within 2 weeks after our representative's inspection. I hope this unfortunate accident will not keep you from having merchandise shipped by Rosemount Corporation Transport in the future.

Yours sincerely,

(Raghu K.)
Customer Relations Deptt.,
Rosemount Corporation

About Short Supply of Goods

Mr. Rustam Bataliwala,
1, Goodluck Street,
Lucknow.

5th January 2004

To,

S. Sindhu Singh Mauji,
Proprietor,
Plastic Bags Ltd.,
Allahabad.

Dear Sir,

Thank you for an early execution of our order. We, however, regret to say that the consignment was found to be short of 5 kilograms of plastic bags. It contained only 45 kilograms of plastic bags, whereas the order was for 50 kilograms of goods.

It could be an act of over-sight. We shall greatly appreciate if you please make up for the loss by an early dispatch of 5 kilograms of plastic goods or credit the amount of 5 kgs of goods to our account. We expect prompt action.

Yours faithfully,

(Rustam Bataliwala)

About Wrong Supply of Goods

Mrs. Geetha Wadhwa,
5, Gurdial Singh Lane,
Guru-ki-Nagri,
New Delhi.

27th January 2004

M/s. Golden Saree Emporium,
Connaught Place,
New Delhi.

Dear Sir,

Last week I visited your showroom and bought about ten Benarasi Silk Sarees, which were considered to be of very good quality. But on reaching home, as I opened the box, which was packed by your salesman, I found that nine conformed to the standard I have demanded. There was one cotton saree not even worth Rs. 100/-. I may point out that I paid for ten Benarasi Sarees. One saree appears to have been packed by your salesman by mistake.

I request you to please look into the matter and replace the wrong saree soon.

An early reply will be very much appreciated

Yours faithfully,

(Geetha Wadhwa)

Reply to the Above

M/s. GOLDEN SAREE EMPORIUM
New Delhi – 1.

7th January 2004

Dear Mrs. Wadhwa,

We thank you for your letter of 27th January and much regret that packing handed over to your was short of Benarasi Saree. We have conducted the necessary enquiry and found that it was by sheer mistake that one saree was misplaced by our salesman. He has also expressed regret. In fact he had pointed out the mistake just after you left our shop. We did not have your postal address or else we would have informed you.

We understand just how you must have felt when you opened the packet.

Please bring the cotton saree and get it replaced at our emporium on any date convenient to you. We assure you of our best co-operation always.

Yours faithfully,
For M/s. Golden Saree Emporium

(Ashok Jain)
Partner

Refusal to Accept Goods

Mr L Kapoor,
234, 1st Main Road,
M G Road,
Lucknow.

M/s Sri Aromatic Cigars Traders,
4/A, Ranigunj,
New Delhi.

30th June 2004

Dear Sir,

The cigars ordered from you on 23rd June were received yesterday, but to my regret I have to write to you that the four half boxes of cigars are not according to order. I stipulated that they should be light and mild, but instead two of the boxes are very dark in colour and strong in flavour. I cannot make use of these, especially as I still have a sizable stock of dark colour cigars.

I am extremely sorry to have to return the 2, 000 cigars. I shall be glad if you will substitute light coloured cigars for them as early as possible.

Yours faithfully,

(L Kapoor)

Replace Offering Special Allowance

SRI AROMATIC CIGARS TRADERS
4/A, Ranigunj,
New Delhi.

2nd July 2004

Dear Sir,

It is with great regret that I learn from your letter of the 30th June, that a portion of my consignment of cigars is not to your satisfaction.

I was away traveling and request you to excuse the mistake of my forwarding clerk. The consignment of light colours in substitution of the four boxes refused by you will leave here in a few day.

I wonder if you can use the four boxes of dark colours? I shall be pleased to make you a special allowance of 15% and hope that you will be able to find a customer for them.

I trust that you will accept my proposition, and that the mistake which has occurred will not deter you from placing further orders with me.

Yours faithfully,
For Sri Aromatic Cigars Traders

(Kedar Nath)
Partner

Asking for A Credit Note—I

S & S BOTTLING PLANT
Daryagunj.

Amrish Machineries,
Patna.

10th April 2004

Dear Sirs,

On 22nd March you delivered to us a Bottle Filling Machine which, after careful examination, we found was not complete. We reported this fact to you on the 23rd March and stated that our fitters were prepared to put the machine in working condition, to which you agreed.

The work has now been completed and the cost to us has been Rs. 500/- and we should be glad if you would send us a credit note for this amount.

This delay in getting the machine into operation has caused considerable inconvenience to us and we hope that every effort will be made in future to see that machines are not sent to us again in an incomplete condition.

Yours faithfully,

Partner

Reply to the Above

AMRISH MACHINERIES
Patna
S & S BOTTLING PLANT
Daryaganj.

15th April 2004

Dear Sirs,

Thank you for your letter of the 10th April informing us that the cost to you of carrying out the necessary repairs to the Bottling Machine supplied on 22nd March was Rs. 500/- we now enclose our credit note regarding this.

We very much regret that you had received one of our well-known machines in an incomplete condition and we assure you that we are thoroughly investigating the matter and that we will take every reasonable precaution to prevent a recurrence of this.

Yours faithfully,

Manager

Asking for A Credit Note—II

SAUHARDA BOOK STORE
West of Chord Road,
Bangalore.

4th June 2004

M/s. T & N Publishers,
Peacock Street,
Jaipur.

Dear Sir,

Thank you very much for your letter dated 30th May 2004. We have returned today the following books by passenger train:

1. Dance Master: 2 Copies
2. Music Master: 3 Copies
3. Novel (My Marriage): 30 Copies

The R.R.No. PN-24378910 dated 4.6.2004 is enclosed to enable you to take delivery of the books.

Please issue us a credit note against the return of the above books to be adjusted against the next order.

Thank you.

Yours faithfully,

Proprietor

Reminder for Credit Note

T & N PUBLISHERS
Peacock Street,
Jaipur.

20th June 2004

Sauharda Book Store,
West of Chord Road,
Bangalore.

Dear Sirs,

This is regarding our letter dated 4th June which also enclosed the R.R. for the returned books. You must have received the books by now.

Much time has lapsed, but you have so far not issued us the credit note. Please treat the matter as urgent and send us the credit note as early as possible.

Yours faithfully,

Proprietor

Credit Note Sent

T & N PUBLISHERS
Peacock Street,
Jaipur.

24th June 2004

Sauharda Book Store,
West of Chord Road,
Bangalore.

Dear Sir,

We sincerely regret the delay in sending you the credit note for the books you have returned. We are enclosing Credit Note No 123 dated 23rd June 2004.

Please acknowledge receipt of the credit note.

We look forward to your next order and assure you of our cooperation.

Yours faithfully,

Proprietor

Replacement of Product
Adjustment Letter—I

MM TOYS LTD.
Lonavala Estate, Mumbai.

Mrs J Sodhi,
8, 1st Cross, 7th Block,
M G Road, Pune.

12th March 2004

Dear Mrs. Sodhi,

We are sending you a new "Barbie" doll by courier, so that you can have it for your daughter's birthday.

We regret very much that the doll came to you in damaged condition. All the dolls are inspected at the factory before they are packed in cartons. However, on rare occasions a package gets unusually rough treatment in shipping and some damage results. Your new "Barbie" received extra cushioning to avoid any possibility of breakage.

Will you be good enough to return the damaged doll to us by parcel post addressed with the enclosed label, which also carries the proper postage? A damage report, filed out according to the facts described in your letter, is also enclosed. We would like you to sign it and return it in the business reply envelope for our insurance record.

I am sure your daughter will be thrilled with "Barbie" and that the doll will bring her many hours of joy.

Yours faithfully,
For MM Toys Ltd

Marketing Manager

Rejecting Defected Products
Adjustment Letter—II

KODAK FUJI LTD.
No. 3, Classic Complex, Bandra, Pune.

Mr. Vijay Raj Chaudhary,
6, Convent Garden,
Nainital.

24th July 2004

Dear Mr. Chaudhary,

I know just how you must have felt when the first films taken with your new camera came back out of focus. It is a real disappointment when a good shot goes wrong.

Because I wanted to make certain that I was doing the right thing. I took your letter to our technical department as soon as I received it. They examined the films carefully and feel certain the trouble lies in your lens adjustment.

Rather than ask you to return the camera to us, they suggest that you take it to a local dealer, Tandon Bros, at 128 Roshanara Street, in your city. I am writing to him, requesting that he make any adjustment necessary and bill us for his services.

After he has made the proper adjustment, I am sure, you will find your camera everything you hope for.

Yours sincerely,

Manager

Complaint Against Baby Food Products

AMUL BABY FOOD PRODUCTS LTD.
45, Penya Industrial Area, Bangalore-5.

Tele: 080 2415 2153
Fax: 080 5214 4256
e-mail: shashidhar@amul.com

M/s. Lloys World Ltd.,
No. 7, VV Mohalla,
Opp: Post Office,
Jayanagara,
Mysore-2.

24th August 2004

Dear Sirs,

We had ordered 2000 kg tins of Nihal Baby Food Powder under our order No. M-4006/PP dated 4 December 2003. Today when the consignment arrived we checked its contents and found only 1500 tins, out of which 45 were badly damaged. It seems on of the cases was not packed properly or some heavy load had been placed over it in transit.

There is a great demand for this powder in the town at this time of the year and we expected to clear the whole stock during the next two months. But it appears some of our customers will have to be disappointed.

With enormous resources at your command we hope can save the situation by sending 500 tins immediately by quick transit service.

As regards the damaged tins, we want your advice. There are two alternatives: either you allow us to sell them at reduced price in which case we shall adjust the total amount realized after deducting our usual commission of 7 per cent or permit us to return them to you at your cost for replacement.

We would very much appreciate an early reply.

Yours faithfully,

(R. L. Bagchi)
Purchase Manager

Mistake in Account

NAVARATHANA TRADERS
No. 45, Mannar's Market, Mysore—1.

M/s.Kangaroo Pins Limited,
No. 451, Industrial Suburb,
Mysore – 7.

Dear Sir,

Thank you for your letter No. TP/463 of 4 January 2004 forwarding Bill No. M 437 dated 4 November. In it you have included two items which we did not buy. They are:

Punching machines 6 Nos. Rs. 54.60
Gum bottles (big) 1 Doz. Rs. 88.80

It seems there has been some mistake in copying from our personal account maintained by you. Will you please get it checked and send us another bill? I am returning here with your bill No. M 437. According to our calculation only Rs. 409.44 are due from us.

Yours faithfully,

(A. Alam)
Office Manager

Asking for Replacement of Cement

BHARAT ALUMINIUM CORPORATION
303, Jahangir Road,
Ahmedabad–380 003.

10 September 2004

Your Reference: Letter No. 43-PA of 4 September
Our Reference: POC-30 U

The General Manager,
Shahi Cement Company Limited,
Sarangpura,
Ghaziabad – 201 001.

Dear Sir,

I regret to inform you that out of 500 bags of cement you supplies, 25 have arrived in damaged condition. They cannot be used at all in construction work. It appears the damage was caused due to inadequate protection against rains. Our storekeeper pointed this out to the truck driver immediately after unloading and he has given a signed note, accepting this position. I am enclosing this note for your information.

I shall be grateful if you will kindly make necessary adjustment in the bill. If, however, you are making supplies to some else in this city in the near future, you may send us the replacement.

Yours faithfully,

(N. Kamath)
Purchase Officer

Requesting for Correct Amount of Cheque

KALRA ENGINEERING WORKS
5/44, Bhagat Singh Marg, Ludhiana—141 001.

14 September 2004

The Financial Manager,
National Development Corporation,
22 Mahatma Gandhi Road,
Bombay – 400 055.

Dear Sir,

Thank you for your letter No. TR-43/30008 of 5 September, 2004. Your cheque No. P4387 of 4 September, 2004 is for Rs. 1959.00 whereas our Bill No./ KLW 10057 of 20 August, 2004 was for Rs. 1995.00 it appears to be a copying mistake the writer of the cheques has reversed the last two digits.

I am sorry to bother you for a small amount but you will appreciate that we have to account for the goods supplied. I, therefore, hope you will not mind sending another cheque for the correct amount. I am returning your cheque No. P 4387.

Yours faithfully,

(B.B. Tandon)
Materials Manager

Adjustment in Account for Excess Purchase Order

KALRA ENGINEERING WORKS
5/44, Bhagat Singh Marg, Ludhiana–141 001.

The Financial Manager,
National Development Corporation,
22 Mahatma Gandhi Road,
Bombay – 400 055.

30/06/2004

Dear Sir,

Please accept our apology for having shipped merchandise in excess of your purchase order.

We have made an adjustment in your account to reflect this error and have arranged for DHL Courier to pick up the excess merchandise on 24/07/2004.

We are sorry for the inconvenience this has caused you and are most appreciative of your cooperation and understanding in this matter. Thank you for your recent order.

Thank you.

Yours faithfully,

Manager

5
REMINDER LETTERS

Reminder letters are written in order to remind the receiver to take action. These letters are brief and refer to the previous letter(s) which have remain unanswered. Sometimes a series of reminders have to be sent, varying in tone from mild to threatening to take action.

Reminder for C Forms

SREE SHIVA PLASTIC COMPANY
Mysore.

20/07/2004

M/s. Sundrop Refiners,
Mumbai.

We wish to remind you that we are still awaiting your reply to our letter dated 2.07.04 pertaining to the notice issued by the government regarding the "C" form for the year 2002-2003. This is now urgently required for our Sales Tax Assessment is going on.

Thank you.

Yours faithfully,
For Sree Shiva Plastic Company

Manager

Reminder for Samples

NEW ESSENTIAL OILS LIMITED
Mysore.

20/07/2004

M/s. Fragrance Limited,
New Delhi.

Dear Sir,

We should be grateful if you could let us have your answer to our letter of 12.7.2004 requesting of samples of essential oils as soon as possible.

Thank you.

Yours faithfully,
For New Essential Oils Limited

Managing Director

Reminder for Plastic Containers

SUNDROP REFINERS
Mumbai.

M/s. Sree Shiva Plastic Company.
Mysore.

10/07/2004

Dear Sir,

As the information requested in our letter of 5.07.04 pertaining to the availability of water tight plastics container is urgently required, your early reply will be greatly appreciated.

Thank you.

Yours faithfully,
For Sundrop Refiners

Purchasing Manager

Reminder for Catalogue

MS. NEHA MATHUR
Queen Fashion House,
Mumbai.

M/s. Lakme India Private Limited,
Mumbai. 02/07/2004

Dear Madam,

We received your letter of the L/01 dt. 27/06/2004 in which you unfortunately omitted to enclose your catalogue. Please send the same.

Thank you.

Yours faithfully,
For Queen Fashion House

Manager

First Reminder for Payment

TOPAZ BLADES LTD.
Mumbai.

29/04/2004

M/s. Kim Kim Dealers,
New Delhi.

Dear Sirs,

We would like to remind you that a sum of Rs. 2, 223.20 remains overdue in spite of a lapse of two months since we dispatched 1, 200 packets of Topaz Blades to you.

We shall be glad if you will send us a cheque immediately. If by any chance your cheque is already in the mail, please ignore this reminder and accept our thanks.

Yours faithfully,
For Topaz Blades Ltd.,

Manager

Second Reminder—An Appeal for Cooperation

TOPAZ BLADES LTD.
Mumbai.

05/05/2004

M/s. Kim Kim Dealers,
New Delhi.

Dear Sirs,

We had written to you on 9th February about the outstanding balance in respect of 1, 200 packets of Topaz Blades amounting Rs. 2, 223.20 which has probably escaped your attention.

We value your business, and we want you to know that you are our privileged customer. We assure you of our continued good service in exchange for prompt payment.

Yours faithfully,
For Topaz Blades Ltd.,

Manager

Third Reminder—An Enquiry

TOPAZ BLADES LTD.
Mumbai.

12/05/2004

M/s. Kim Kim Dealers,
New Delhi.

Dear Sirs,

We very much regret that we have not received any reply to our letter dated 05/05/2004 regarding the over-due amount of Rs. 2,223.20 from your firm.

We have failed to understand why you have not sent any reply in spite of the lapse of more than three months since we dispatched the packets of Topaz Blades to you.

It is regrettable that our letters have been ignored which may jeopardise our business relations.

We shall appreciate an immediate reply.

Yours faithfully,
For Topaz Blades Ltd.,

Manager

Fourth Reminder—Threatening Legal Action

TOPAZ BLADES LTD.
Mumbai.

27/05/2004

M/s. Kim Kim Dealers,
New Delhi.

Dear Sirs,

We very much regret that the sum Rs. 2,223.20 has been overdue since long and in spite of our repeated requests and reminders you haven't cared to reply or remit the amount.

If we do not receive the above amount within a week of the receipt of this notice, we shall be constrained to resort to legal proceedings and you shall be held liable for the consequences.

Yours faithfully,
For Topaz Blades Ltd.,

Manager

Letter for Payment

KASHIWAL PLASTICS LIMITED
234, Subhash Shinde Road,
Churchgate,
Mumbai–400 029.

15 December 2003

The Manager,
Dagar Enterprises,
472A, New Rohtak Road,
Bhiwani – 125 021.

Dear Sir,

I am sending a copy of the statement of account dispatched to you on 30 November 2003. The draft for Rs. 55,000/- for the supply of 200 suitcases has not yet been received.

Please expedite payment.

Yours faithfully,

(P. K. Saxena)
Credit Manager

Reminder for Payment

KASHIWAL PLASTICS LIMITED
234, Subhash Shinde Road,
Churchgate,
Mumbai–400 029.

31 December 2003

The Manager,
Dagar Enterprises,
472A, New Rohtak Road,
Bhiwani – 125 021.

Dear Sir,

This is our third attempt to collect Rs. 55,000/- that you owe us for the 200 suitcases supplied to you on 10 November 2003. No action seems to have been taken on our statement of account sent to you on 30 November and our reminder of 15 December.

We had readily agreed to your terms of credit and it is only fair that you honour them. If perchance our earlier communications have escaped your attention, I am sure this one will reach you and evoke a prompt response.

Yours faithfully,

(P. K. Saxena)
Credit Manager

Reminder for Immediate Payment

KASHIWAL PLASTICS LIMITED
234, Subhash Shinde Road,
Churchgate, Mumbai– 400 029.

15 January 2004

The Manager,
Dagar Enterprises,
472A, New Rohtak Road,
Bhiwani – 125 021.

Dear Sri Ram Das,

Before I come to the purpose of writing this letter, let me wish you and your firm a prosperous New Year.

As you know, we supplied 200 suitcases of different sizes to your firm on 10 November 2003 and for this supply a sum of Rs. 55,000/- was to be remitted to us in early December. But despite three communications, we have not so far received the payment.

We do not in any way wish to damage your credit reputation. I am aware that your value your just as we do ours. But any more delay on your part may force us to a still avoidable course of action.

I should therefore be grateful if you could kindly send the amount by demand draft immediately on receipt of this letter.

Yours faithfully,

(P. K. Saxena)
Credit Manager

Letter Threatening Legal Action

KASHIWAL PLASTICS LIMITED
234, Subhash Shinde Road,
Churchgate,
Mumbai–400 029.

23 February 2004

The Manager,
Dagar Enterprises,
472A, New Rohtak Road,
Bhiwani – 125 021.

Dear Sri Ram Das,

This is inform you that unless the demand draft for Rs. 55,000/- is not received by 7 March, 2004, we shall place the matter in the hands of our legal adviser for necessary action.

Yours faithfully,

(P. K. Saxena)
Credit Manager

6
SALES LETTERS

The objectives of a sales letter are:

(a) It introduces new goods in the market more effectively, quickly, at a lower cost and in a wider area.

(b) It introduces the salesman to the prospective customers even before the former has called on them because it reaches them earlier and thus keeps them informed.

(c) It widens the market for existing products without much cost.

(d) It educates the customer in selecting the right type of goods. It keeps the customers constantly in touch with the company and its products and service.

Points to Remember

Begin the letter in a striking manner in order to arouse the reader's curiosity and tempt him to read further. Give a vivid description/explanation of the product, service and proposition being offered. Make an appeal to the reader by telling him how the article benefits him. Convince the reader by giving evidence. Induce the reader to act at once by offering different types of inducement or by forceful and convincing words.

Furniture Sales

DURO FURNITURE STORES
(Manufacturers and Dealers of Steel and Wooden Furniture)
Royal Road, Vilas Nagar, Mysore.

1st May 2004

Mrs. Anjali Shahasrabudhe,
Price Street,
Kailas Nagar,
Bangalore – 5.

Dear Madam,

Life is hard and competition is tough. But DURO Easy Chairs are soft and luxuriously comfortable.

Life in this century sometimes seems shallow, but DURO Easy Chairs are deep.

Sometimes things seem harsh and the world appears to reject you. But DURO Easy Chairs embrace your, relax your, make you look on the brighter side of thins.

DURO Easy Chairs fir handsomely into any home. They have a simple, comfortable-looking construction that fits happily with your furniture.

Under the beautiful, glowing fabrics are cancelled specially-constructed pillows over a light aluminium and leather-webbing frame. The chairs are so light that even a ten-year girl can easily move them from place to place.

Expensive? You be the judge. DURO Easy Chairs start at Rs. 35. This is possible only because we are manufacturing them in large numbers realising that they are most popular chairs in our State.

DURO Easy Chairs are on display at all City Furniture Show Rooms in your city. Visit the nearest store and just try sitting in one today. You will say, "I must own DURO Easy Chair".

Yours sincerely,
For Duro Furniture Stores,

(M. Vishnukant)
Sales Correspondent

Gift Articles for Sale

SHYAM'S GIFT CENTRE
Ramnagar Colony,
Indore–3.

10th October 2004

Mrs. Padma Joshi,
8 (C) Tagore Nagar,
Indore – 5.

Dear Mrs. Joshi

Roses are red
SHYAM's is gay,
Look what's ahead,
HAPPY NEW YEAR DAY!

Have a New Year Gift problem? Then let us think for you, for we have quite a few ideas to help you solve your Gift problem.

We are sure you like to make that day, 20th October—the NEW YEAR DAY—a most Happy Day through your intelligent selection of gifts that will keep articulating your affectionate thoughtfulness the year round. How about this suggestion-beautifully embroidered and colourfully designed frocks for babies; skirts for the lasses; manly fashioned ultra-modern dresses for the lads; and thoughtfully tailored trousers for the gentlemen—all patterned in assorted sizes, colours, designs and styles.

In facts, every section of each of the three SHYAM'S stores of your city has new, modern, pleasing and most practical gifts for all occasions and for all types of people: young and old, men and women. Nay, you can also depend on your SHYAM'S store for an exhaustive stock of most up-to-date, fashionable articles of all types for the use of those gentlemen, ladies, girls and boys who care so much for their dress and appearance at home and outside.

Why not visit your nearest SHYAM'S store for glimpse of our attractive stock? You can even contact us over the phone or mail your order and we serve you for not only your New Year Day but everyday requirements in the year.

Cordially Yours,

(C.K. Naidu)
Sales Correspondent

Sale of Paint

INDIAN PAINTS COMPANY
Chartered Building.
Fort, Mumbai–1.

July 8, 2004

Colours to please you,
Colours to brighten you,
Colours to match your every mood,
INDIAN PAINTS have them,
Add Colour to your life,
B(u)y INDIAN PAINTS.

Dear Madam,

Give your home a personality. Your home can be a heaven of peace and serenity. It can be cheerful and gay, full of light and space, it can express your personality and reflect your good taste–all with colour. Make colour turn your house into a home you will be proud to live in and friends will be delighted to visit.

INDIAN PAINTS have mass appeal.

We strive to make quality that masses can afford and classes admire. **Indoplast**—to cite an example—is such a product. This Ṣatin-finish paint for walls is priced to fit in small budgets. It took us five years to develop this revolutionary product. Before it was marketed, it had been tested on sites for over two years. Technology and enterprise pressed into service of the common man is so satisfying.

INDIAN PAINTS have PROTECTIVE COATS,

INDIAN PAINTS give a perfectly uniform, durable and bright finish that never patches or peels. INDIAN PAINTS offer,

ECONOMY in use—because they have high covering capacity—you need less quantity to cover larger areas flawlessly.

WASHABILITY—you can easily wash off dust, dirt and stains with soap and water,

NON-FADING, NON-PEELING, PERFECTLY UNIFORM FINISH—because they have quality—tested ingredients.

HIGH GLOSS & DURABLE FINISH—because they are odour-free and dry quickly.

For best result select your colours from 55 exquisite shades. Will so many shades to choose from, you could have hundred of colour schemes to brighten up your sweet home.

Would you ask for our catalogues which offer a riot of most fascinating colours? You will surely be tempted to give INDIAN PAINTS a trial test. You have an easier way. Check with your contractor, ask him for advice and INDIAN PAINTS Shade Cards.

Colourfully yours,

(B. Black)
Sales Correspondent.

Insurance Policy Scheme

JEVAN JYOTHI GRATUITY PROVIDENT CORPORATION
No. 45, Vinoda Complex,
JC Road, Bangalore-2.

Tel.: 2154112

Ms. Ashish Mathur,
No. 45, 7th Cross,
9th Main, Jayanagar,
Bangalore- 4.

Dear Sir,

What do your employees want when they retire? Financial security, don't they?

We know you already have contributory provident fund and gratuity schemes. Give one more benefit and rank among the very few progressive business houses which take special for of those who work for them.

A group insurance scheme to suit organizations like your— this is what we offer. Under this scheme each employee will contribute a small sum from his monthly salary. It will be collected by your office and sent to us. And in return we guarantee to pay an attractive sum to each member when he retire to his family if he dies while in service. The main features of the scheme are its low premium and a convenient way of payment. For details, Please go through the enclosed folder.

At present the scheme is being introduced in a few towns only. Our agent is likely to visit your town some time in April. Please suggest a convenient date and time for him to call on you. He will be happy to explain further details and answer any questions you may have to ask. He will also assist you in going through the formalities.

To give us an opportunity to serve you, please fill in the enclosed reply card and mail it today.

Yours faithfully,

(T.P. Sohal)
Divisional Manager

Sale of Grinder

SUHANI GRINDER INDIA PRIVATE LIMITED
No. 7, Opp: Prabha Talkies, Mysore-12.

Mrs. Shyamala Sharma,
No. 45, 8th Cross,
Kuvempunagar, Mysore. 22/05/2004

Dear Sir,

We have manufactured a perfect answer to all your kitchen problems—the Suhani Domestic Grinder.

Simple to use, unique in design, it can grind within minutes pepper, chillies, grams, pulses, *dalia, pithi,* etc. and help you prepare your favourite dishes without sweat and toil. Now you need not postpone the preparation of dishes which your children love and your husband adores. Buy a Suhani today and add new cheer to your life.

As you will see from the enclosed pamphlet, there are three models for you to choose from Popular, Deluxe and Royal and each one available in three colours, namely, ash grey, sky blue and light mustard. Tell us which one you want by filling in the enclosed order form and we shall send it by V. P. P. If you wish to pay in advance, please send us, by M.O. or crossed cheque Rs. 65 plus Rs. 5.40 for postal charges along with the order and become the proud owner of a gadget which will become the talk of your neighbourhood.

Yours faithfully,
For Suhani Grinder India Private Limited.

(P.K. Suredeep)
Sales Manager

Sale of Catalogues

MYSORE TARPAULINS
D.D. Urs Road, Mysore.

M/s. Roshni Tarpaulins,
Mysore. 25/04/2004

Dear Sir,

The Mysore Tarpaulins Catalogue came into existence in 2000 and in four short years has become one of the most successful catalogues on the market. For this, we are pleased, proud and grateful.

We are pleased because our customers have confirmed our belief that if the products we offer are new, exciting, innovative and of excellent quality, they will be purchased.

We are proud because we know we are a company that keeps its word to its customers, that guarantees that any merchandise can be returned within 30 days if it proves to be disappointing in any way, and that always lets our customers know if there is to be a delay in delivery.

We are grateful to customers like you, because you confirm our beliefs that fine service and quality results in satisfied customers. Without you, there would be no reason to be pleased or proud. We thank you for your orders and for giving us the opportunity to be of service to you.

Our special summer catalogue is at the printers and should be in your home soon. We hope that you will be pleased with our new selections.

Thank you.

Yours faithfully,
For Mysore Tarpaulins

Partner

Sale of Catalogues

MYSORE TARPAULINS
D.D. Urs Road, Mysore.

M/s. Roshni Tarpaulins,
Mysore.

27/04/2004

Dear Sir,

This is my favourite kind of letter. How many letters have I had to write over the years advising you of a price increase? Why, you ask, am I so happy? Read on.

This is to advise you that, for a limited period of time, we are reducing prices on certain items in our catalogue. Take a moment to review the enclosed catalogue. I have circled in red ink the items that are temporarily reduced.

What an opportunity!

Please take advantage of these prices. If you wish to order large quantities, or stagger shipments, give me a call and we will try to work out mutually acceptable terms and conditions. In any event, get your order in, as these prices are only in effect until 25/05/2004.

I do enjoy writing this type of letter. Thank you in advance for your order.

Yours faithfully,
For Mysore Tarpaulins

Partner

Apologies for Unexpected Delay

MIHEER EXPORT PRIVATE LIMITED
Sector 45/15, Industrial area, Mumbai.

Tele: 412 025541
Fax: 412 512562
e-mail: miheer@export.com

15/04/2004

M/s. Morico Fashion House,
Bordeaux,
Len Sen,
France.

Dear Sir,

Thank you for your order. At this time we cannot fill your order due to an unexpected shipment delay from our overseas suppliers.

We will hold your order for arrival of the merchandise, and ship shortly thereafter. Unfortunately, we cannot provide you with a specific shipping date at this time.

Thank you for your anticipated patience in this matter.

Yours faithfully,
For Miheer Export Private Limited.

(P.K. Mehta)
Export Executive

Apologies for Unexpected Delay

MIHEER EXPORT PRIVATE LIMITED
Sector 45/15, Industrial area, Mumbai.

Tele: 412 025541
Fax: 412 512562
e-mail: miheer@export.com

23/07/2004

M/s. Morio Glass House,
Nice, Len Sen,
France.

Dear Sir,

This is to inform you that we are unable to make delivery on the above referenced purchase order on the date indicated.

We should have our merchandise ready to ship within 10 days of the original delivery date and we hope that you can hold off until that time.

We did want to inform you of this delay as soon we were advised in order to give you as much time as possible to make alternate arrangements, if necessary. We can assure you, however, that if your order remains in force we will expedite delivery to you as soon as we have received the merchandise.

Please accept our apology for this delay and thank you for your understanding.

Yours faithfully,

(Mahesh Takkar)
Sales Manager

Change of Price

PROCTER AND GAMBLE INDIA PRIVATE LIMITED
No. 2, Sansad Marg,
New Delhi.

Tele: 00 0143 251 2544
Fax: 00 0143 256 2551

M/s. Sumith Simth India Limited,
No. 45, Sector 2,
Noida.

23/06/2004

Dear Sir,

Due to the increase in raw material costs, we must unfortunately raise the cost of our merchandise to you.

We have avoided raising our prices for as long as possible, but we can no longer prolong the inevitable. We have enclosed our new price list for your review which goes into effect on 12/07/2004 Any orders placed between now and 12/07/2004 will be honored at the lower prices.

We wish to thank you for your valued account and know that you will understand the necessity for this price increase.

Yours faithfully,

For Procter and Gamble India (P) Ltd,

(Krishnaswamy Iyer)
Managing Director

Refusal for Allowing Discount

PROCTER AND GAMBLE INDIA PRIVATE LIMITED
No. 2, Sansad Marg,
New Delhi.

Tele: 00 0143 251 2544
Fax: 00 0143 256 2551

M/s. Sumith Simth India Limited,
No. 45, Sector 2,
Noida.

23/04/2004

Dear Sir,

In the past twelve months you have purchased a considerable amount of merchandise from us, which pleases us greatly.

Since you have never taken advantage of the 2% discount we offer for early payment, we thought that you might be unaware of just how substantial your savings could be. The savings on last year's purchases alone would have amounted to Rs. 12,000/-.

By paying us within 10 days of delivery, you can actually save 24% of the face amount of your average monthly bill over the period of a year. There are, in fact, firms who prefer to borrow funds to take advantage of this discount.

Of course, you know what is best for your own business, but we want to be sure that you are aware of this savings factor.

We would like to take this opportunity to thank you for the orders you have given to us over this past year and the promptness with which you have always paid. It is a pleasure doing business with your firm.

Yours faithfully,
For Procter and Gamble India Private Limited,

(Krishnaswamy Iyer)
Managing Director

Short of Payment

GOGIA FRAGRANCES
No. 45, Andheri Nagar,
Andheri East,
Mumbai-5.

Tele: 0143 2251 1154
Fax: 0143 2561 2546
e-mail: gautham@gogia.com

M/s. Nard Essence Private Limited,
No. 45, 7th Cross,
Kalpataru Road,
Chennai-7.

Dear Mr. Arjun,

Your cheque made payable to Nard Essence Private Limited in the amount of Rs. 17,750/- has been returned to us for insufficient funds. The bank will not allow us to redeposit the cheque since it has already been presented on two occasions.

Would you please bring the amount of the cheque, plus Rs.150.00 fee for our service charge for returned cheques, to the manager's office at:

Nature Care Solutions
MG Road,
Bangalore,
Karnataka

We must ask that this amount of Rs. 17,900 be paid by either cash, certified cheque, or money order.

If you have any questions, you can contact me at the above telephone number during office hours.

Thank you.

Yours faithfully,
For Gogia Fragrances

(Gautham Bakshi)
Accountant

Thanking for Payment

GOGIA FRAGRANCES
No. 45, Andheri Nagar,
Andheri East,
Mumbai-5.

Tele: 0143 2251 1154
Fax: 0143 2561 2546
e-mail: gautham@gogia.com

M/s. Nard Essence Private Limited,
No. 45, 7th Cross,
Kalpataru Road,
Chennai-7.

23/04/2004

Dear Sir,

Your letter of 18/04/2004 in which you enclosed your payment of Rs. 7,500/- has been received and I would like to thank you for your prompt remittance following our telephone call of the same date.

Thank you for the kind words contained in your letter. We look forward to many years of mutual prosperity.

Yours faithfully,

(Gautham Bakshi)
Accountant

Defect in Material Supplied

GODREJ INDIA PRIVATE LIMITED
No. 26, Sector 74/A1, Industrial Area,
Penya, Gujarat.

Tele: 4152 4251

M/s. Seaport Shipping Corporation,
Kovalam, Cochin.

23/07/2004

Dear Sir,

It has been our policy in the past to supply ice to our customers when their ice machine has broken down. Because we have many customers who are paying later and later, we are forced to set down stronger company policies. Our new policy will go into effect from August 3, 2004, and is as follows:

1. If the customer is more than 15 days late in their monthly payment and the machine is not working, we will not supply ice. We will repair the machine, and the number of days in which the machine has not been in service will be credited to the customer's account. At the time of our service call we will expect payment in full of any unpaid balance due us.
2. There will be a sur-charge on accounts falling more than 30 days behind.

While I am sorry that we must go to such extremes as those outlined above, I am afraid that there is no alternative. Our company policy is, and always has been, to provide the best service available to our customers. We can only continue to do this with our customer's cooperation.

If there are any questions regarding our new policy, please give me a call.

Thank you.

Yours faithfully,
For Godrej India Private Limited,

(Rajesh Godrej)
Asst. Manager

Apology for Delaying in Refunding

GOGIA FRAGRANCES
No. 45, Andheri Nagar, Andheri East,
Mumbai-5.

Tele: 0143 2251 1154
Fax: 0143 2561 2546
e-mail: gautham@gogia.com

M/s. Nard Essence Private Limited.
No. 45, 7th Cross,
Kalpataru Road, Chennai-7

27/04/2004

Dear Sir,

After reading your letter of 24/07/2004, I can thoroughly understand why you are running out of patience.

While it would be easy to place the blame on our computer, this poor fellow has received enough abuse since joining our firm. After all, he only follows the orders that are given to him. Therefore, please accept my apology for the delay in refunding your money for Rs. 2100/-.

Our bookkeeping department has been instructed to issue a cheque to you at once, which you should be receiving within a few days.

I am grateful that your letter was brought to my attention and I appreciate your perseverance in settling this matter.

Once again, I am very sorry for the inconvenience this has caused you.

Thank you.

Yours faithfully,
For Gogia Fragrances

(Gautham Bakshi)
Accountant

Apology for Delay in Delivering Goods

KIRAN GLASS WARES
No. 22, Mannar's Market,
Mysore-7.

M/s. Pushkaani Glass House,
No. 2, 8th Cross,
Kumratunga Road,
Colombo.

27/06/2004

Dear Sir,

This is to inform you that we are unable to make delivery on the above referenced purchase order on the date indicated.

We should have our merchandise ready to ship within 10 days of the original delivery date and we hope that you can hold off until that time.

We did want to inform you of this delay as soon we were advised in order to give you as much time as possible to make alternate arrangements, if necessary. We can assure you, however, that if your order remains in force we will expedite delivery to you as soon as we have received the merchandise.

Please accept our apology for this delay and thank you for your understanding.

Thank you.

Yours faithfully,
For Kiran Glass Wares

(Kiran Virani)
Marketing Manager

Change of Address

KIRAN SALES CORPORATION
401, Vinobha Complex, Sayyajirao Road, Mysore-570 02.

M/s. Pushkaani Glass House,
No. 2, 8th Cross,
Kumratunga Road,
Colombo.

30/07/2004

Dear Sir,

As of Monday, July 1, 1986, Kiran Sales Corporation of Indian's Eastern Regional Office will be located in our new offices and warehouse building at 401 Vinobha Complex, Sayyajirao Road, Mysore–570 002. The telephone number for this new location is (0821) 255-5428.

Our Manufacturing Division will remain at 2550 Sector 73/A, Hebbal Industrial Area, Bangalore.

I have enclosed our most recent brochure on robotic equipment for your review. I hope you find it interesting.

Thank you.

Yours faithfully,
For Kiran Sales Corporation

(Kiran Virani)
Marketing Manager

Change of Address

RANGSONS ELECTRONICS
Hebbal Industrial Area, Hebbal, Bangalore.

23/05/2004

M/s. Cyber Electronics Private Limited,
No. 47, Yadavagiri Industrial Area,
Unit 5, 11th Main,
Yadavagiri,
Mysore–5.

Dear Sirs,

As our new letterhead indicates, we have recently changed the name of our business from M/s. Rajalakshmi Electronic Company to Rangsons Electronics.

There has been no change in management and we will be providing the same products and fine service on which we have built our reputation in the industry. We would appreciate it if you would bring this announcement to the attention of your accounts payable department and direct them accordingly.

Thank you for being one of our valued customers. We appreciate your cooperation in this matter.

Thank you.

Yours faithfully,
For Rangsons Electronics

(Manoj Kaushik)
Asst. General Manager

In Absence of Responsible Person

HARIHAR AND SUGANDH
No.4451, Darya Ganj, New Delhi.

M/s. Haripriya Sugandh Co.,
No.5, 7th Cross, 8th Main,
Kuvempunagar,
Mysore–12.

25/06/2004

Dear Sir,

Because Mr. Ramachandra is out of the office for the next two weeks I am acknowledging receipt of your letter dated May 20, 2004. It will be brought to his attention immediately upon his return.

If I may be of any assistance during Mr. Ramachandra's absence, please do not hesitate to call.

Thank you.

Yours faithfully,
For M/s. Harihar and Sugandh

(Ravishankar V.)
Asst. Manager

Asking Order for Advertised

NEW WELL DONE FURNISHURES
(Furniture Manufacturers)
428, Opp. Hima Canteen, Hebbal Industrial Area,
Hebbal, Mysore.
Telephone 251 51 97; Fax 251 51 98

Your ref: MO/AA
Our ref: PT/RO

Mr M. Muralidharan Pillai,
Furniture Unit,
Neel Kamal Furniture House,
15, Andheri West, Mumbai. 15 September 2004

Dear Mr Pillai,

We were very pleased to receive your letter in answer to our advertisement for sofas and armchairs and, as requested, enclose a copy of our latest catalogue. A set of sample materials is being sent under separate cover.

You may be particularly interested in our latest "Today" range which is proving very popular with our customers. The sofa is easily converted into a comfortable double-bed and the armchairs are supplied with matching cushions. You will find particulars of our terms in the price-list printed in the catalogue.

We very much look forward to a trial order. It will enable you to see for yourself the high quality of the material and finish.

Thank you.
Yours sincerely,

(Sadashivaiah Panchaksh)
Managing Director

Encl.: 1 Catalogue

Sales Letters

M/S. RAMESH PUBLISHING HOUSE
4457, Nai Sarak, Delhi–110 006.

Tel: 23918938, 23918532

Mr Krishna Rao Apte,
No.15, Shanthiniketan,
7th Main, Big Bazar Street,
MUMBAI.

21/07/2004

Dear Sirs,

Please find enclosed the latest literature and samples of our new range. I have also included a display kit for your window or counter which you may want to test out at your premises in Reims.

You will find additional information on prices, discounts, incentives and marketing Materials for your sales staff.

I hope all goes well and look forward to extra orders in the near future.

Thank you.

Yours faithfully,
For Ramesh Publishing House

(Nitha Mathur)
Publicity Manager

Packing & Transport

T.K. GHOSH & COMPANY
Sikkim.

30 January 2004

M/s. Sushil Bros & Co.,
Parade Road,
Assam.

Dear Sirs,

We have received your letter of 5th January. All the containers are clearly marked with the accepted international sign-fragile-top-bottom. We thank you for your order.

Yours faithfully,

(Lokesh Panchaksh)
Manager

Despatch Details

JYOTI TRADING CO.
Church Road, Chennai.

M/s. Haripriya Sugandh Co.,
No.5, 7th Cross, 8th Main,
Kuvempunagar, Mysore–12.

12 August 2004

Dear Sirs,

Following your letter of 8th August, please find enclosed the details concerning the shipment of our order No A/175.

Each article must be packed in special cases to avoid all risk of damage during transport.

Please deliver the goods to our shipper's warehouse and send the invoice in duplicate.

Yours faithfully,

(Jayanth Balaiah)

Gift Offer for Purchasing any Electrical Items

SUHANI GRINDER AND ELECTRICAL CO.
Opp: Ranjith Talkies, Mysore Main Road, Mysore.

Mrs. Sujatha Basu,
No. 2, 8th Main Road,
Vani Vilas Puram,
Mysore–1.

29/07/2004

Dear Customer,

I just wanted to personally write and thank you for your recent purchase. I'm sure you'll be very pleased with your new Grinder purchased for many years to come.

And because this is your FIRST purchase from us, I wanted to do something special to show my appreciation. Here's what I had in mind: For the next 30 days if you need any Electrical items, I'll give you 1 box of Utensil or 1 Pressure Cooker for FREE for every 3 you buy.

Thank you.

Yours faithfully,
For Suhani Grinder and Electrical Co.,

(Subhas Ghosh)
Sales Manager

7
BANK LETTERS

A bank is a financial institution. In today's ever-expanding commercial field, banks have become indispensable on account of the multi-dimensional services performed by them. They provide loans, lake deposits and offer facilities for withdrawal of money through cheques. The over-draft facility offered by the banks to various commercial firms sustains business. This advancing money for commercial purposes, collecting money against the cheques issued, discounting of the Bill of Exchange, railway receipts and securities, issuing letter of credit, providing foreign exchange etc. fall under the category of essential functions that the bank perform.

While drafting such letter to banks, the customer should try to be brief, to-the-point and accurate.

Given in the following pages are some specimen bank correspondence.

Opening a Current Account

To,

The Manager,
Indian Bank,
Main Branch,
Ashoka Road,
Mysore. 15/07/2004

Dear Sir,

We wish to open a current account in the name of M/s. Raja & Bros, a registered firm.

Please let us know about the formalities which have to be completed before such an account is opened in your branch.

Yours faithfully,
For Raja & Bros

Authorised Signatory

Reply to the Above

M/s. Raja & Bros.,
Mysore. 16/07/2004

Dear Sirs,

Please refer to your letter dated 15th July 2004. We are enclosing the requisite application forms, which may please be filled up and brought to the office on any working day so that the account may be opened.

We assure you of our best services.

Yours faithfully,
For Indian Bank

Manager

Request for a Cheque Book

SRIRAM MOTORS
124a, Sriharsha Road
Mysore.

The Manager,
Indian Bank,
Main Branch,
Ashoka Road,
Mysore. 15/07/2004

Dear Sir,

We shall thank you very much if you please send us a cheque-book containing 100 bearer cheques through our representative, Miss Neelam Sud, the bearer of this letter.

Attested signatures of Miss Sud are given below:

Yours faithfully,

(B Jaiprakash)
Manager

Specimen Signatures

Returning a Dishonoured Cheque

INDIAN OVERSEAS BANK
Prithvi Arcade, Ashoka Road,
Mysore.

July 11, 2004

M/s Kiran Corporation,
Mysore.

Dear Sir,

We regret to say that your Cheque No. 514115 dt. 06/07/2004 drawn in favour of Shir Kumaralila for Rs. 5250/- has been returned because of insufficiency of funds in your account. The balance to your credit as of today stands at Rs. 3250/- only.

It is always better to retain sufficient amount in balance to meet such contingencies. If need be, you may apply in advance for an overdraft for which the usual securities have to be produced in time.

Yours faithfully,
For Indian Overseas Bank

Manager

Reply to the Above

KIRAN CORPORATION
Mysore.

19/07/2004

Dear Sir,

Reg: **Dishonoured Cheque No. 514115 dt. 06/07/2004**

I fail to understand why the cheque issued in favour of Shri Kumaralila for Rs. 5250/- was dishonoured. I had sent a cheque for deposit on 7th May for an amount of Rs.11,000/- thus raising the balance considerably. Enough time was allowed for collecting the amount against that cheque.

Please look into the matter to find out why the earlier cheque was not got encashed.

I look forward to your reply.

Yours faithfully,
For Kiran Corporation

Authorised Signatory

Request for Overdraft Facilities

TINMIN MANUFACTURERS PRIVATE LIMITED
Prempura, Ram Singh Nagar,
New Delhi 110 005.

November 1 2004

The Manager,
Punjab National Bank Ltd.,
New Delhi–110 001.

Dear Sir,

To boost our sales during the Diwali season, we have planned to place large orders for toys and other such goods as are generally required by the customers during these days of festivities. We shall require overdraft facilities for Rs. 500,000/- during the period ranging from August 15 to September 15, after which we shall be in a position to keep our account in credit.

We propose to deposit as security 15 shares of Bajaj Motors Ltd., the present market value of which is more than Rs. 20,00,000/-. We do hope that the security offered will be considered to be sufficient for the grant of an overdraft facility.

We look forward to an early response.

Yours faithfully,
For Tinmin Manufacturers Private Limited

Manager

Standing Instructions Issued to a Bank

Mr Hari Prasad,
2, Gulzari Lal Nanda Lane,
Kurukshetra.

January 5, 2004

To,

The Manager,
The Lakshmi Commercial Bank Ltd.,
Kurukshetra.

Dear Sir,

I request you to please make the following periodical remittances until I write to the contrary:

1. Rs. 250/- per month to the Life Insurance Corporation of India on the 10th of every month.
2. Rs. 1000/- quarterly to Mr. Dindayal Rao, 5, Naqlilane, Sonepat (Haryana).

I am enclosing the standing order form filled and signed as desired by you. Please debit all the incurred to my amount.

Thank you.

Yours faithfully,

(Hari Prasad)

For Stop Payment of a Cheque

Mr Rajinder Singh,
1, Blue Sky Lane,
Gurgaon (Haryana).

15th June 2004

The Manager,
The New Bank of India Ltd.,
Gurgaon.

Dear Sir,

We had issued a cheque No. PLK/1234567 to Shri Udho Dass of M/s. Amita Ink of Gurgaon, but the person concerned has not been able to fulfill all the requisite conditions.

Therefore we request you to please see to it that the cheque may not be encashed unless we report to the contrary.

Thank you.

Yours faithfully,

(Rajinder Singh)

Enquiring About the Fixed Deposit Rates

Smt Radha Bai,
1, Mohan Singh Tower,
New Delhi.

June 1, 2004

The Manager,
The Indian Bank Ltd.,
New Delhi–3.

Dear Sir,

I wish to invest a sum of Rs. 15,000/- in fixed deposit for a period of two years in your bank. Will you please write to me the rates of interest regarding this.

An early response will be highly appreciated.

Yours faithfully,

(Radha Bai)

About the Loss of Pass Book

Mr Banarasi Lal,
22, Maheshwari Road,
Allahabad,

July 1, 2004

The Manager,
New Bank of India Ltd.,
Allahabad.

Dear Sir,

I have a Savings Bank Account No. 34215 with your Bank. I lost my passbook while traveling in the train yesterday.

I request you that a new pass book may please be issued to me. Please write to me if I am required to do anything regarding this.

An early response will be highly appreciated.

Yours faithfully,

(Banarasi Lal)

For the Transfer of Savings Account

Mr Lalit Kumar Sharma,
20, Tulsi Nagar,
New Delhi – 5.

June 2, 2004

The Manager,
Allahabad Bank Ltd.,
Gurgaon.

Dear Sir,

Reg: **Transfer of my Saving Bank Account No.**

I wish to say that I have been maintaining an account referred to above with your Gurgaon Branch for the last nine years. As I am shifting to Tulsi Nagar, a New Delhi suburb in the vicinity of Connaught place, New Delhi, I am unable to maintain my account with your Branch at Gurgaon.

I request you to please transfer my account to your New Delhi Branch as early as possible.

I am giving below my previous and present address for your ready reference:

Previous Address:

Gurdev Nath Aggarwal,
Sadar Bazar,
Gurgaon.

Present Address:

Gurdev Nath Aggarwal,
20, Tulsi Nagar,
Connaught Place,
New Delhi.

Please write to me as soon as you complete the formalities.

Thank you.

Yours faithfully,

(Lalit Kumar Sharma)

For Cancellation of an Issued Cheque

NAVODAYA PRINTERS AND PUBLISHERS
Ranigunj,
New Delhi.

August 1, 2004

The Agent,
State Bank of India Ltd.,
New Delhi.

Dear Sir,

Ref: **No. 123-72**

Our cheque No. P-123456 dt. July 26th 2004 for Rs.4,000/- issued in favour of M/s. Bhagwan Dass & Co., has been lost in transit.

We request you to please treat the cheque referred to as cancelled. Please do not pay to any person who present the cheque in your branch. We have issued a fresh cheque Y-765412 for Rs. 4,000/- to M/s. Bhagwan Dass & Co., which fact may please be noted.

Thank you.

Yours faithfully,
For Navodaya Printers and Publishers

(Sri Kishen Talreja)

For Receiving Wrong Draft

GULMOHAR & CO., LTD.
Putli Ghar, Lucknow.

July 1 2004

The Agent,
State Bank of India Ltd.,
Lucknow.

Dear Sir,

Ref: **VIP-1**

We regret to say that we have received a Draft No. 0046789 dated 26.6.2004 for Rs 5000/- today by mistake. We fail to understand how it has been sent to our firm, instead of sending it to M/s. Gulab Ram Aggarwal & Co. Our draft for Rs 20,000/- in favour of G R Enterprises, Chennai is pending with you.

We are enclosing the draft. Please acknowledge when you receive it.

We request you to please expedite our draft.

Thank you.

Your faithfully,
For Gulmohar & Co. Ltd.,

(Muralidhar)
Finance Manager

Encl.: One Draft.

Mistake in Account

SETHI & SONS
Faizabad.

8 March 2004

The Manager,
Canara Bank,
College Road, Faizabad.

Dear Sir,

We have received the Pass Book for our current account No. 1084. we regret to say that our account has been debited with Rs. 6125/- on 24 February 2004. We have checked all our records and also our cheque book, and have found this entry incorrect.

Please look into the matter immediately and effect necessary corrections for which the pass book is being sent.

We expect an immediate action.

Yours faithfully,
For Sethi & Sons,

(P C Sethia)

Applying for a Bank Loan

SHWETA TRADING CO.
Asansol.

14th November 2004

The Manager,
Central Bank Ltd.,
Asansol.

Dear Sir,

We are interested in getting a loan of Rs. 250,000/- against mortgaging our landed property worth Rs. 10 lakhs. The loan is required for a period of 10 months.

We shall be glad to have your terms as early as possible.

Yours faithfully,
For Shweta Trading Co.

(Badrinath S)
Partner

Sending R/R through Bank

DEVILAL & CO.
Gol Bazar, Haryana.

4th June 2004

The Manager,
Canara Bank,
R.K. Puram, Delhi.

Dear Sir,

We are sending our invoice No. 141 along with R/R No. AG 16789 and request you to realise the amount from the firm concerned through the State Bank of India, Jhansi, and credit the amount to our account. The bank charges will be paid by the firm.

Yours faithfully,

(Devidayal Singh)

Encl.: Invoice, R/R

Issue of Trade Advance

CENTURION BANK LTD.
268/A, Lal Bazar,
Mahatma Gandhi Road,
Ahmedabad.

To,

M/s. Shah Auto Mart,
Seventh Main Road,
Ahmedabad.

06/04/2004

Dear Sir,

Sub: **Issue of Trade Advance.**

Please find enclosed herewith a Demand Draft of Centurion Bank Ltd., bearing No. 8777 dated 05/04/2004 for Rs.8 Lacs favouring M/s. Shah Auto Mart payable at Ahmedabad towards Trade Advance.

Kindly acknowledge the same and revert the acknowledgement to us.

Thank you.

Yours faithfully,

Bank Manager

Trade Advance Renewal Letter

SHAH AUTO MART
Seventh Main Road,
Ahmedabad.

Date: 02/04/2004

Centurion Bank Ltd.,
Ahmedabad.

Dear Sirs,

Re: **Renewal of Trade Advance**

In connection with our Letter of Acceptance of Trade Advance dated 02/04/2004 we request you to renew the Trade Advance as and when the advance amount becomes Nil by virtue of loan agreements from our dealership/ amount repaid by us.

The letter of acceptance of trade advance facility shall continue to apply to all such trade advances disbursed against this renewal letter.

Thank you.

Yours faithfully,

(Rithik Shah)

Grant of Trade Advance

CENTURION BANK LTD.
268/A, Lal Bazar,
Mahatma Gandhi Road,
Ahmedabad.

2nd April 2004

Mr. Rithik Shah,
M/S. Shah Auto Mart,
Ahmedabad.

Dear Sir,

With reference to the discussion we had, we are pleased to grant an advance of Rs. 8 Lacs as Trade Advance to you for a period of 30 days, Interest at the rate of 13% p.a. will be charged for the first 20 days and thereafter at the rate of 13% p.a. for the next 10 days (i.e. 21st day to 30th day). You are expected to liquidate the advance in 30 Days, interest at the rate of 21% p.a. will be charged.

The following document will have to be executed for providing TRADE ADVANCE.

1. Acceptance of trade advance on Rs. 100/- stamp paper duly signed by the dealer in the manner specified.

We accept the above terms and conditions.

Yours faithfully,

Bank Manager

Acceptance of Terms and Conditions of Bank for Loan

BHANDARI TRADING COMPANY LIMITED
234/A, Chandni Chowk, Delhi.

11 September 2004

The United Commercial Bank Limited,
1133, Mahatma Gandhi Road,
New Delhi – 110 014.

Dear Sir,

Please refer to your letter No. C-BC/43 of 4 September, 2004.

We are grateful that you have agreed to advance a sum of Rs. 20, 000/- (Rupees Twenty Thousand only). The terms and conditions you mention are acceptable to us. We shall send our accounts officer to sign the agreement at 11 a.m. on Monday, 16 September, 2004 as you suggest.

Yours faithfully,

(A.S. Bowmick)
Secretary

Apology for Wrongly Credited

GLOBAL TRUST BANK LIMITED
Devraj Urs Road,
Mysore.

Ms. Kanchana Walia,
14, Kanthraja Urs Road,
Kuvempunagar,
Mysore.

15/04/2004

Dear Madam,

Thank you for your recent correspondence regarding your account number 9150. We were able to track down the error and have credited your account accordingly. A report to this effect has also been sent to our credit reporting company.

As of this date, your account balance is Rs.34,250/-.

You are a valued customer and we apologize for any inconvenience this mix-up may have caused. If we may be of further assistance please contact this office at your convenience.

Thank you.

Yours faithfully,
Anthra Trust Bank Limited

Manager

8
APPLICATION LETTERS

This section presents many different ways to design and write application letters. In many job applications, you attach an application letter to your resume. The letter comes *before* the resume.

The role of the application letter is to draw a clear connection between the job you are seeking and your qualifications listed in the resume. To put it another way, the letter matches the requirements of the job with your qualifications, emphasizing how you are right for that job. The application letter is not a lengthy summary of the resume. It selectively mentions information in the resumé, as appropriate.

Common Sections in Application Letters

Introductory paragraph

That first paragraph of the application letter is the most important; it sets everything up—the tone, focus, as well as your most important qualification. Avoid diving directly into work and educational experience in the introductory paragraph. Alternately, you can do the following:

- State the purpose of the letter—to inquire about an employment opportunity.

- Indicate the source of your information about the job—newspaper advertisement, a personal contact, or other.
- State one eye-catching, attention-getting thing about yourself in relation to the job or to the employer that will cause the reader to want to continue.

You do these in the space of very short paragraph—no more than 4 to 5 lines of the standard business letter.

Main body paragraphs

In the main parts of the application letter, you present your work experience, education, training—whatever makes that connection between you and the job you are seeking. Remember that this is the most important job you have to do in this letter—to enable the reader see the match between your qualifications and the requirements for the job.

There are two common ways to present this information:

- *Functional approach*—This one presents education in one section, and work experience in the other. If there were military experience, that might go in another section. Whichever of these section contains your "best stuff" should come first, after the introduction.
- *Thematic approach*—This one divides experience and education into groups such as "management," "technical," "financial," and so on and then discuss your work and education related to them in separate paragraphs.

Closing paragraph

In the last paragraph of the application letter, you can indicate how the prospective employer can get in touch with you and when are the best times for an interview. This is the place to urge that prospective employer to contact you to arrange an interview.

Points to Remember

- The application should be so written that it stimulates enough interest and curiosity and creates a desire in the mind of the prospective employer to see you personally.
- Write respectfully and modestly but frankly, stating your qualification without boasting or under-rating.
- Show your confidence in being able to handle the job efficiently.
- It is better to avoid making a mention of the salary one expects, except where it is otherwise asked.
- If you are employed do not use the letterhead of that firm or company for writing the application.
- Give your reasons for wanting to leave your present position, where necessary.

Given in the following pages are some specimen application letters.

Application for Science Editor

MS. PUSPHA BHARGAVI
245, 9th Cross, Gokulam II Stage
Mysore – 570 002.

July 24, 2004

Central Food Technical Institute,
24, Dhanvanthri Road,
Mysore.

Attn: **HR Dept, Req #56234**

Dear Sir,

I am writing in response to your ad in the *Times of India* for a position of Science Editor. I believe my broad-based scientific knowledge and writing skills make me an excellent candidate for this position.

My education includes a B.S. in Zoology with honors, and two years of medical school. Through these studies, I have gained in-depth knowledge of many scientific subjects which include biology, chemistry, anatomy, physiology, and genetics. As an Advanced Placement English student, a participant in University Interscholastic League writing contests, and the daughter of an English teacher, I have a good working knowledge of English as well as strong writing skills. Currently, I am enrolled in a technical communications course to further augment my writing skills.

Concerning my related experience, I have been employed as a Science Consultant and Technical Writer for Education Networks Corporation. In that position, I was the sole writer on scientific subjects (life and earth sciences) for a project involving development of software for *Compton's Children's Encyclopedia* on CD-ROM. My teaching experience includes tutoring medical and nursing students in human anatomy, physiology, and histology. Positions working in the medical field have allowed me to develop superior interpersonal skills.

I plan to use my employment in the medical field and my technical writing experience to find full-time employment as a writer on technical subjects and more fully utilize my scientific knowledge. I will also continue evening coursework in technical communications and desktop publishing.

Enclosed is a resume that provides more detail about my background. I am excited by an opportunity such as the one you advertised, and I believe I would be a creative and energetic asset to your organisation.

Yours sincerely,

(Puspha Bhargavi)

Encl.: Resume

Application for Programmer

Mr. Mahesh Prasad,
1103, 7th Cross, 3rd Main,
Jayanagar, Bangalore – 560 009.

August 5, 2004

The Personnel Assistant,
Indian Overseas Bank,
P.O. Box 112, Chennai.

Dear Sir,

I am writing about your advertisement in the *'The Hindu'* of August 1st 2004, for the post an experienced programmer in the database environment. I believe that I have the qualifications and experience that you are looking for.

As for my experience with database programming, I have worked for the past year as a programmer/analyst in the Query database environment for Advanced Software Creations. In that capacity, I have converted a large database that was originally written in a customized C language database into the Query database environment. I am currently working on a contract with AB Software Ltd to make major modifications to its existing Query database application. On both of these assignments, I have also served as customer contact person.

My resume is enclosed, for additional information on my background and qualifications. I would welcome a chance to talk further with you about the position you have advertised for. I can be reached by phone between 9:00 a.m. and 6:00 p.m. at (080) 2515-197.

Yours sincerely,

(Mahesh Prasad)

Encl.: Resume

Application for Quality Assurance Manager

Mr Muthaiah Chengappa,
724, 10th Cross, Gokulam II Stage,
Hyderabad 500 023.

19 January 2004

Director of Personnel,
South Region Aerospace,
Udakamandala,
Nilgiris.

Dear Mr. Karthar Singh,

Please consider me as an applicant for the position of Quality Assurance Manager in the Military Division there at South Region Aerospace. I have extensive knowledge of military contracting and substantial Quality Assurance background.

I have spent the last 12 years with the Department of Defence administering contractual quality requirements at Defence contractor facilities such as South Region Aerospace. In this position, I have had the opportunity to function in all areas of Quality Assurance.

In December 1995, I will receive an Associates degree in Applied Science from Kochin Community College with a major in Quality Assurance Technology. I passed the Indian Society for Quality Control certification exam for Quality Engineering and am certified as a Quality Engineer as December 1995. In the Department of Defence, I am certified in the Quality Assurance area including Electronic Commodity, Mechanical Commodity, Nuclear Commodity, and NASA. Additionally, I am certified in all of the nondestructive test disciplines.

Enclosed is a resume that provides a more detailed listing of my background and qualifications. I am confident that I possess all the necessary qualifications for the position and am ready to meet with you at your convenience. You can reach me at (0821) 2515-197 between the hours of 7:00 a.m. and 5:00 p.m.

Yours sincerely,

(Muthaiah Chengappa)

Encl.: Resumé

Application for Programmer

MS SUJATHA RAJKUMAR
83, 11th Cross, 4th Cross,
OPP: Pragathi Bakery,
Kuvempunagar, Mysore.

July 4, 2004

The Personnel Manager,
Personnel Department,
Cyber Cafe,
P.O. Box 178,
Kuvempunagar, Mysore.

Dear Madam,

I am writing in response to your newspaper ad in the July 2 edition of the *Indian Express* concerning your need for a Programmer/Analyst III. I believe that I have the qualifications, experience, and enthusiasm that you are looking for.

As for my work experience, I have been employed with two organizations over the past three years that have drawn on my computer-programming skills. My work at Loganis Mortgage Corporation involved the setup of new software, training of personnel, and the direct use of AutoCAD on a 10-user LAN. I worked as an assistant programmer at HydroLogics Corporation, doing much of the same design, code, and test work as the regular programmer/analysts. In December, I will graduate with a Bachelor of Science from Mysore University I have studied and developed a thorough understanding of the following programming languages: Pascal, Assembler, COBOL, RPG, and C.

You will find enclosed with this letter a copy of my resume which provides a much more detailed description of my education and employment history. I would welcome an opportunity to talk with you further about the Programmer/Analyst position.

Yours sincerely,

(Sujatha Rajkumar)

Encl.: Resumé

Application for Sales Manager

2/3, Kutub Place,
Mehrauli,
Delhi–30.

10th April 2004

M/s. Supreme Builders and Traders Ltd.,
New Delhi.

Dear Sir,

I learnt that your reputed firm requires the services of a Sales Manager and that you have been in search of an energetic and dynamic young man suitable for the job. I am confident that I can fulfil the requirements of the job and wish to submit my application for your consideration.

For the last ten years I have been working as a sales representative with M/s Loopmier Ltd., Pul Bangash, Delhi-5, a firm manufacturing cables and electronic goods. I have been performing my job very satisfactorily and twice I earned special annual increments for my efficiency and dedication, as the testimonials annexed show.

In this organization, my duties mostly related to the training of the sales personnel and organizing market research and sales promotion in the company. Although I am enjoying working here, being an ambitious youth, I have been looking forward to an opportunity to rise in life.

In view of the reputation that your firm possesses and my keenness to work in my neighbourhood in Mehrauli, where the production unit of your firm is located, I approach you with the request that I may be given a chance to serve your firm as a Sales Manager. My long ranging experience in the trade is an asset which shall prove beneficial to your company.

As regards my qualifications, I did my B. Engineering from Lucknow University in 1983. Since then I have been working with one firm or another as a Sales Executive.

I am a young man of 36 years with robust health and amiable attitude.

If given a chance, I assure you that I shall prove diligent and honest in the execution of duties entrusted to me.

I look forward to a favourable response.

Yours faithfully,

(Rajesh Bhat)

A Positive Reply

M/S. SUPREME BUILDERS & TRADERS LTD.
New Delhi.

22nd April 2004

Dear Mr. Rajesh Bhat,

Please refer to your unsolicited enquiry for the job of a Sales Manager. Please call on the undersaid on any convenient day next week between 12.30 p.m. and 2.30 p.m. in the business premises. He shall be glad to interview you for the post, as a vacancy has occurred very recently.

Please write to us about the time and date when it is convenient for you to visit our premises.

Yours sincerely,

Personnel Manager

A Negative Reply

M/S. SUPREME BUILDERS & TRADERS LTD.
New Delhi.

22nd April 2004

Dear Mr. Rajesh Bhat,

I appreciate your request for the post of Sales Manager in our firm, but I regret to say that at present there is no vacancy and there is little chance of such a vacancy occurring soon.

However, I may assure you that when a vacancy occurs, we shall advertise for the post and then you may contact us.

Thank you.

Yours sincerely,

Personnel Manager

For the Post of a Private Secretary

Ms. Sujatha Mehta,
10, Mortand Road,
Calcutta.

23/04/2004

The Managing Director,
Orient Fans Ltd.,
Calcutta.

Dear Sir,

I have come to know that your private secretary is quitting her job, as she is migrating to England to settle there.

I wish to offer myself as a candidate for the post and submit the following for your consideration.

I am a graduate from Shantiniketan University and have got a good command of the English language. I know typing and shorthand. I can easily type at a speed of 45 words per minute and my shorthand speed is approximately 110 words per minute.

It has been my ambition to join a big firm and gain experience. I shall be very grateful if you give me an opportunity to work under you. I assure you that I would do my best to give you all the satisfaction you expect from a private secretary.

Thank you.

Yours faithfully,

(Sujatha Mehta)

9
REFERENCE LETTERS

Reference letters are also called recommendation letters. They are used by a person when applying for a new job. While writing a reference letter start by describing how long you've known the person and in what capacity. Include dates of employment and details on how you've worked with (or known) the person.

Continue by describing the person's skills and performance and what makes them an ideal candidate for a potential new employer. Also include two or three outstanding attributes. End by summarizing why you are recommending this person for employment. You may also want to provide a phone number or E-mail address so employers can follow up if they have questions or want more information.

M/S. BHARAT ENGINEERING COMPANY,
No. 212, 8th Main, Gokulam,
Mysore–570 002.

February 1, (2004)

To Whom it May Concern

I've been Kiran's manager at Bharath Engineering Company for almost four years. It was my pleasure to promote Kiran to mechanical engineer II last year, because he consistently meets and often exceeds his job requirements.

Kiran is an enthusiastic, dedicated employee with reliable work habits. He often does not need guidance or supervision, but willingly accepts it when offered. He is consistently successful in improving his skills, and he works hard to do so.

Kiran is always willing to pitch in to help the team, and he gets the job done right the first time. He is efficient in planning projects; punctual in meeting deadlines; and conscientiously adheres to company standards and guidelines.

You'd be hard pressed to find an employee more dedicated than Kiran, and I recommend him as a reliable addition to your engineering staff. If you'd like more information, I'd be happy to provide it. Please call the phone number above and ask for me by name.

Sincerely,

(Krishna Swamy)
Manager, Mechanical Engineering
krish@leoengineering.com

M/S. BHARAT ENGINEERING COMPANY
Khanapur Road,
Belgaum.

Tel.: 2515197
Fax 2515198

February 1, 2004

To Whom it May Concern

I've been Karuna's manager for over six years. While I wish her only the best and fully understand that she must advance her career, I'm truly sorry to see her go. It has been a pleasure having her on my team.

Karuna is a professional technical writer of the highest calibre, who meticulously researches, formats, edits and proofs her documents. I've received many compliments from customers who rely on Karuna's documentation. Management and personnel in tech support, engineering, technical training, and other departments praise her work.

Karuna is an innovative self-starter, who rarely needs supervision. She is punctual and typically exceeds expectations. She handles pressure well, and will voluntarily work overtime and take work home to meet a deadline. For example, we received a rush order from one of our customers for a complex product modification, including critical user documentation. Holly not only made the extremely tight deadline, but beat it; yet she still produced a stellar, technically-accurate addendum for the standard user manual. Sales, marketing, training and engineering were quite pleased with Holly's performance in this crunch. Even our CEO was impressed, and our customer was ecstatic. This is just one example among many of Karuna's superior skills and admirable work ethics.

Karuna is an invaluable asset to any technical communications department, and I highly recommend hiring her. If you'd like to discuss her attributes in more detail, please don't hesitate to contact me.

Sincerely,

(Usha Singh)
Manager,
Technical Communications
Ext. 245,
usha@technocom.com

CYBER TECHNOLOGIES, INC.
24, KT Street, 5th Cross,
Hyderabad.

Ph: (040) 555-0000
Fax: (040) 555-0001

February 1, 2004

To Whom it May Concern

Ajay Jadeja worked for me at Pratham Technologies for three years, as a senior technical instructor. I am writing this letter of recommendation to confirm that his recent layoff from Pratham Technologies was not in any way tied to his performance, and to highly recommend him as an employee with your organization.

Had I been given the choice, I would not have laid Jadeja off. But it was not my decision to make. Pratham Technologies decided to withdraw from the PC market, balance expenses with the anticipated reduction in sales revenue, and hire a consulting firm to evaluate long-term staffing needs. As a result, Pratham Technologies drastically reduced the size of its workforce by dissolving the entire PC division, including the technical training department. Unfortunately, this major reorganization left no other position open for Jadeja. We regretfully had to let him go.

Jadeja is a conscientious, highly-skilled technical instructor, worthy of at least a senior or management position. He has keen insight into the learning process, and is an expert in needs analysis, project management, course development, and classroom instruction. Jadeja's in-depth product knowledge, unique instructional techniques, and excellent people skills have consistently received rave reviews from his students. Should conditions at XYZ Pratham Technologies change, I wouldn't hesitate to hire him back.

If you would like to speak to me about Jadeja's skills, talents and work habits, feel free to call (040) 2515197 or page me by dialing (040) 22515197.

Sincerely,

(Prashanth Jain)
Vice President, Pragathi Technical Services
prashanth@pragathi.com

10
RESIGNATION LETTERS

Writing a letter of resignation may be an unpleasant task, but there's really not that much to it. In its simplest form, you just date your letter of resignation, say when and what you're resigning, sign it and hand it over.

Resigning from the post of Asst. Manager

KOWSALYA.S
238, 8th Cross, Gokulam III Stage,
Mysore – 570 002.

Phone: 2515197; Fax phone: 2515197
E-mail id: kowsalya@sancharnet.in

13th July 2004

Aditya Computers,
227, Vani Vilas Puram,
Opp. Police Station,
N R Mohalla, Mysore.

Dear Sir,

Sub: **Resignation Letter**

Please accept this letter as my formal notice of resignation from Aditya Computers, effective [15th July 2004, two weeks from date above]. The associations I've made during my employment here will truly be memorable for years to come.

I hope a two-week notice is sufficient for you to find a replacement for me. If I can help to train my replacement or tie up any loose ends, please let me know.

Thank you very much for the opportunity to work here.

Sincerely,

(Kowsalya.S)
Asst. Manager

CC: Accounts Department

Resigning from the Post of Asst. (Administration)

LAKSHMI S.
227, Vani Vilas Puram,
Opp: Police Station, N R Mohalla

Phone: 2515197
Fax: 2515197
E-mail id: koush@vsnl.com

13th July 2004

The Manager (Administration),
M/s. Cavinkare Private Limited
321, Sector 9,
Kattukopam,
Pondicherry.

Dear Sir,

Sub: **Resignation**

Effective two weeks from the date of this letter, I resign my position as Assistant (Administration).

I've enjoyed working here. Thank you very much for the opportunities you've provided.

Sincerely,

(Lakshmi. S)

Cc: *Manager (HRD)*

Resigning from the Post of Marketing Executive for Better Opportunity

ANIL KUMBLE
37, 4th Cross, 9th Main, Jayanagar,
Bangalore–560 005.

Phone: 080-2555 2323
Fax: 080-2555 2323
E-mail id: anil@vsnl.com

July 13, 2004

The General Manager,
M/s. Bata Shoe Company (I) Pvt. Ltd.,
27, M G Road, Bangalore-560 006.

Dear Madam,

Sub: **Resignation**

Please accept this letter as my notice of resignation, effective 15th July 2004.

This wasn't an easy decision, because I am grateful for the rewarding employment I've had with M/s. Bata Shoe Company (I) Private Limited. But after long hours of consideration, my decision is now final and I have accepted a position with another company.

Sincere thanks and best wishes for the future.

(Anil Kumble)
Marketing Executive

Cc: Marketing Department

Resigning from the Post of Cashier

HARSHAD MEHTA
25, Mahagali Street, Andheri West, Mumbai.

Phone: 014 25151971
Fax: 014 25151971
E-mail id: harshad@yahoo.com

25th June 2004

The Managing Director,
M/s. Sriram Finance Corporation,
27, Opp: Andal Goel,
2nd Main, Pudu Kottai,
Chennai.

Dear Sir,

Sub: **Resignation**

This is to formally notify you that I am resigning from M/s. Sriram Finance Corporation as Cashier with effect from 1st of July 2004.

Thank you for the opportunity to work for such an outstanding organization.

Sincerely,

(Harshad Mehta)
Cashier

Cc: Manager

11
CIRCULAR LETTERS

A circular letter is a communication meant to notify or convey to all customers, business friends, shareholders, etc. certain fundamental changes or important information like: changes in the firm's goods, policies, prices, or services; changes in the name of a firm; change of address; admission, retirement, or death of a partner; opening a new branch; issue of bonus shares or debentures; clearance sales, etc.

Opening a New Business

S. SURAJ SINGH & CO.
Cloth Merchants, Arjan Gate, Karnal.

12th November 2004

Sir/Madam,

We are opening a new clothier's business at Arjan Gate Karnal, on the 19th November under the name of the firm as: Suraj Singh & Co.

Large varieties of silken cloth and other fabric including sarees of various type will be available in this shop at comparatively cheaper rates to the customers.

Even readymade clothes will be available and a separate department has been contemplated for these.

Please pay a visit to our premises on any day convenient to you after its opening on the 19th November.

Yours faithfully,
For S. Suraj Singh and Co.,

(Ram Lal)
Manager

Closure of a Branch and its Opening at a New Location

SRINIVASAN FABRICS LIMITED
Sector-2, New Township, Faridabad (Haryana).

5th July 2004

Dear Sir/Madam,

We have been constrained to announce the closure of our business house in Sector No.2, New Township, Faridabad, from the 7th July 2004. Because of various difficulties related to the expansion of our business.

We propose to open our new branch on July 10 in Sector No. 7 where we have constructed a new magnificent and spacious building. Our address shall be as follows:

SRINIVASAN FABRICS LIMITED.
7-B, Sector No. 7,
New Township, Faridabad (Haryana).

All our different varieties of cloth including sarees, readymade garments and other fabric will be available at comparatively cheaper rates.

We shall be glad to welcome you for the opening of the new premises.

Yours faithfully,
For Srinivasan Fabrics Limited,

Proprietor

Opening of a New Branch

THE NEW STATE EXCHANGE BANK OF MYSORE
15, Marine Drive, Mumbai.

Gentlemen,

We have pleasure in announcing that we have opened a branch of our house at the above address for the transaction of Exchange and commission business.

Having had long experience of business of the kind, and being in possession of a very large capital, we can assure you that you may place your orders with us in full confidence.

You will find enclosed a schedule of our charges and a statement of terms both of which, we feel sure, will prove satisfactory to you.

We respectfully solicit a share of your patronage, and assure you that any commissions with which you may favour us shall receive our prompt and most careful attention.

Yours faithfully,

(T. N. Bhaskaran)
Manager

Notifying Price Increase to Retailers

GOVINDRAJ & SONS
D.D.Urs Road, Mysore.

1st April 2004

Dear Sirs,

With effect from May 2004, the prices of all our products will be raised by 10 per cent.

While we regret this increase, the increase is as per All India Trade Association's directives. We assure you that no change in quality of products will be made. This increase has become unavoidable because of the rising costs of labour and production. The new price lists are being prepared and these will be sent to you as soon as they are ready. Meanwhile, to help you with business, we will charge you the old rates on all orders received upto the end of April 2004.

The business you are placing with us is indeed appreciated and you may be sure we will do everything in our power to take the best possible care of your requirements.

Yours faithfully,
For Govindraj & Sons

Partner

Obtaining a New Agency

BIGSTON TELEVISION
Mumbai.

14th August 2004

Dear Sirs,

We are pleased to announce that we have got an agency of "Bigston Television", a world renowned manufacturing firm. Whose television sets are in operation in about 60 countries of the world.

We have already made arrangement for maintaining a big stock of the television sets which will be assembled in our own factory with components supplied by the company, the representatives will stay with to watch the assembling task.

We have been appointed sole agents for distribution of "Bigston Television Sets" throughout the State of U.P.

We are enclosing the price list and we shall give a discount of 20 per cent to the dealer who are interested in procuring television sets from us for sale in their own show rooms in various cities of the country.

We hope that with your patronage we shall be able to maintain the high reputation of our firm. We assure you of the exquisite quality of the television sets to be supplied and we make an offer to you to become our sub-agents.

Thank you.

Yours faithfully,
For Bigston Television

Partner

12
THANK YOU LETTERS

Thank you letters are also called goodwill letters because their purpose is to sell the reputation of a person/ organization. Thank you letters may also be written after attending an interview. These letters serve as reminders and will reinforce the good impression the candidate may have made at the interview.

Thank You for Career Advice

Ms Usha Singh,
30, 11th Cross, 9th main
Gokulam,
Mysore – 570 002.

Phone: (0821) 251 5197
E-mail id: usha@firstbyte.com

February 1, 2004

Ms. Karuna Sharma,
No. 24, Kuvempunagar,
Mysore – 570 002.

Dear Ms. Sharma,

Thank you for talking with me on Wednesday in response to my inquiry about summer internship possibilities in social services in the Jayanagar area. After speaking with you, I think I am much better prepared to pursue internship opportunities.

On your advice, I have updated my resume, emphasizing my recent hotline volunteer activities. A copy is enclosed for you. I also plan to contact Manisha Mehra as you suggested, and appreciate your giving me her name.

Thank you for inviting me to visit your office. I will be in Jayanagar in March, so I will call your office two weeks in advance to see if it would be convenient to schedule a visit.

Again, thank you so much for your help and advice. I look forward to meet with you in March.

Yours sincerely,

(Usha Singh)

Thank You for Application for Job

Mr. Sujit Mehta,
23, 7th Cross, 8th Main
Bannimantap, Mysore–570 003.

Phone: (0821) 251 5197
E-mail id: sujit@vsnl.com
March 30, 2004

Mr. Abhishek Behari,
Akshaya & Associates,
100 ft. Road, Double Road,
Mysore–570 005.

Dear Mr. Abhishek Behari,

Thank you so much for taking time from your busy schedule to meet with me last Tuesday. It was very helpful to me to learn so much about the current projects of Akshaya & Associates and the career paths of several of your staff. I appreciate your reviewing my portfolio and encouraging my career plans. I also enjoyed meeting Ms Nisha Malhotra, and am glad to have her suggestions on how I can make the most productive use of my last semester in college.

Based on what I learned from my visit to your firm and other research I have done, I am very interested in being considered for employment with your firm in the future. I will be available to begin work after I graduate in May 2004. As you saw from my portfolio, I have developed strong skills in the area of historical documentation and this is a good match for the types of projects in which your firm specializes. I have enclosed a copy of my resume to serve as a reminder of my background, some of which I discussed with you when we met.

During the next few weeks I will stay in contact with you in hopes that there may be an opportunity to join your firm. Thank you again for your generous help.

Yours sincerely,

(Sujit Mehta)

Encl.: Resumé

Thank You for Visit to Office

Ms Pooja Bakshi,
909, 4th Street, 5th Cross,
Bangalore–Mysore Road,
Mysore–570 001

Phone: (0821) 215 4566
E-mail id: pooja@yahoo.com

December 1, 2004

Ms. Vanitha Kulkarni,
30, 7th Main Street,
Ooty Road, Jayanagar,
Mysore–570 006.

Dear Ms. Kulkarni,

Thank you so much for your time and advice during my visit to your office last week. I very much appreciate your inviting me to visit since this was my first experience seeing the hands-on work which takes place in a design department. I learned a great deal, and hope to share what I learned with members of our students chapter of the Indian Society of Interior Designers.

After January, I will be in contact with you again to explore the possibility of arranging a summer internship with your firm. As I mentioned to you when we met, I had an opportunity to work on an intense, four-day interdisciplinary project judged by faculty in which my team received top honors. I gained valuable teamwork, problem-solving and presentation skills and learned to work effectively with students studying to enter different professions. I believe my skills would make me an asset to an organization like yours which often must produce excellent work under tight time constraints.

Thank you again for all your help, and I look forward to talking with you in the coming months.

Sincerely,

(Pooja Bakshi)

Thank You for Interview

Mr Ganesh Acharya,
421/12, A Block,
Brindavan Apartments,
Basheer Bagh,
Hyderabad 500 003.

E-mail: ganesh@venus.com

January 26, 2004

Ms. Geetha Rao,
Human Resources Manager,
Fashion Department Store,
Lavelle Road,
Mumbai.

Dear Ms. Rao,

I enjoyed interviewing with you during your recruiting visit on October 25, 2003. The management trainee programme you outlined sounds both challenging and rewarding and I look forward to your decision concerning an on-site visit.

As mentioned during the interview, I will be graduating in December with a Bachelor's degree in Fashion Merchandising. Through my education and experience I've gained many skills, as well as an understanding of retailing concepts and dealing with the general public. I have worked seven years in the retail industry in various positions from Sales Clerk to Assistant Department Manager. I think my education and work experience would complement your management trainee programme.

I have enclosed a copy of my resumé and a list of references that you requested.

Thank you again for the opportunity to interview me with Fashion Department Store. The interview served to reinforce my strong interest in becoming a part of your management team. I can be reached at (040) 222614525 or by E-mail at ganesh@venus.com, should you need additional information.

Yours sincerely,

(Ganesh Acharya)

Encl.: Resume, references

Thank You for Interview

Ms Anusha Kunj,
170, HAL Airport Road,
Opp: Kidschemp, Bangalore – 560 002.

Tel.: (080) 2555-6241
e-mail id: anusha@yahoo.com
March 3, 2005

Ms. Prathima Rao,
Personnel Manager,
Rangsons Computers and Electronics,
1212, Hebbal Industrial Area,
Mysore - 570 006.

Dear Ms. Rao,

Thank you for the opportunity to visit with you and see your facilities last Wednesday. Both the interview and the tour made for an exciting and complete day.

I was particularly impressed with your warehousing procedures. Mr. Nitin was very thorough in explaining the process to me. I will be corresponding directly with him to express my appreciation. Incidentally, the process you use is quite similar to one I have been researching through an independent study this term. Perhaps I can share my final report with you and Mr. Nitin.

The expense report you requested is enclosed.

Again, thank you for your hospitality during my visit and for all your efforts to arrange my visit. Having seen your operation, I am all the more enthused about the career opportunity that Rangsons Computers and Electronics offers. I look forward to your decision.

Yours sincerely,

(Anusha Kunj)

Encl.: Expense sheet

13
E-MAIL

Electronic mail is popularly called e-mail. It is mail sent by electronic means, through a computer. In today's highly technological age, the e-mail is quickly replacing traditional means of communication, i.e. post, fax, etc.

As with all written communications, your e-mails should be clear and concise. Sentences should be kept short and to the point.

This starts with the e-mail's subject line. Use the subject line to inform the receiver of EXACTLY what the e-mail is about. Keep in mind, the subject line should offer a short summary of the e-mail and allows for just a few words. Because everyone gets e-mails they do not want (SPAM, etc.), appropriate use of the subject line increases the chances your e-mail will be read and not discarded into the deleted e-mail file without so much as a glance.

Because e-mails have the date and time they were sent, it is not necessary to include this information in your e-mail correspondences. However, the writing used in the e-mail should be like that used in other business writings. The e-mail should be clear and concise, with the purpose of the e-mail detailed in the very first paragraph.

The body of the e-mail should contain all pertinent information (and should be direct and informative).

Make sure to include any call to action you desire, such as a phone call or follow-up appointment. Then, make sure you include your contact information, including your name, title, phone and fax numbers, as well as snail-mail address. If you have additional e-mail addresses, you may want to include these, as well.

If you regularly correspond using e-mail, make sure to clean out your e-mail inbox at least once each day. Of course, the exception here may be on days you do not work, such as weekends and holidays.

Make sure you return e-mails in a timely manner. This is a simple act of courtesy and will also serve to encourage senders to return your e-mails in a timely manner.

Points to Remember

- Make sure that you fill in the subject line
- Subject should specific; not extremely generic. E.g: Information
- Address depends on Who, When, Relationship. For e.g. Hello, Dear, Good Morning, etc.
- The e-mail should conclude with Thanks and regards
- Contents should preferably focus on one issue
- Capitals are totally forbidden. Use of capitals is equivalent to shouting. Similarly small letters through the e-mail are not acceptable
- Avoid idioms as far as possible
- Pay attention to spelling, grammar, sentence construction
- K I S S: Keep It Short and Simple

E-mail about Notification

From : nk234@yahoo.com
To : ambk23@hotmail.com
Sub : Notification on cost auditor

Dear Mr Badrinath,

Am in receipt of your letters dated 4th Feb 2004. Am sending the notification on cost accounting records as an attachment. Unless the government issues an order for the appointment of a cost auditor, you are only required to maintain the cost records. The notification itself contains detailed instructions on the maintenance of these records.

I hope the above meets with your requirements.

Thanks and regards,

(Nirmal Luthra)

Sending Forms & Minutes

From : sudesh@yahoo.com
To : ambk23@hotmail.com
Sub : Forms and minutes

Kind Attn: Mr Vasudeva,

Am sending the following as attachments:

1. Blank Form 23 and F18
2. Draft minutes of the Selection Committee

Thanks and regards,

(Sudesh Kumar)

Information about Auditors

From : kumar5@rediffmail.com
To : nksharma@yahoo.com
Sub : Auditors

Dear Mr Sharma,

Thanks for your reply.

There is a change in the information what I gave you on your visit. The auditors for the company are APB & Associates for the financial year 2002-03.

Thanks and regards,

(P K Kumar)

Performance Report

From : sundari@eth.net
To : apcoomer23@rampco.com
Cc : bnkumar@rampco.com
Subject: Performance Report of March 2004

Kind Attn: Mr A P Coomarswamy

Thank you for your e-mail. I'm going to Bangalore tomorrow and will be back in the evening. By Saturday afternoon I shall e-mail you all that you require. I do have a soft copy of Performance Report of March 2004 and will send that too.

Thanks once again.
Regards,

(Sundari M)

Thanks

From : apcoomer23@rampco.com
To : sundari@eth.net
Cc : bnkumar@rampco.com
Subject: Performance Report of March 2004

Dear Ms Sundari,

Thanks for your response which is quite comprehensive. I appreciate the trouble you are taking in sending me the Performance Report.

Many thanks for your assistance.

Regards,

(A P Coomarswamy)
Chief Operating Officer
Rampco Ltd.

Meeting in India

From : saralee@intpharma.com
To : nalinis@eth.net
Cc : martin2000@intpharma.com
Subject: Meeting in India

Dear Nalini,

We will be arriving in India on Tuesday, 16th March 2004.

We would like to schedule a meeting at 4.00 pm on Wed 17th at our office in Chennai to discuss the above with you. Please confirm your availability asap.

We would like to meet with you to discuss and sign the necessary documents and agreements pertaining to the purchase of second hand machinery from Germany.

Please let us know if you have other things to discuss with us before end of this week.

Regards,

(Sara Lee)

Follow Up on Above

From : saralee@intpharma.com
To : nalinis@eth.net
Cc : martin2000@intpharma.com
Subject: Meeting in India

Dear Nalini,

In order ensure that our visit is fruitful, please ensure that the following are completed BEFORE our arrival:

1. Draft agreement
2. Drawings of the electrical installation
3. A meeting scheduled with the engineers at 6 pm on the 17th March
4. Bank papers are ready for signature

Please reply item by item ASAP.

Your urgent reply is appreciated.

Regards,

(Sara Lee)

Reply to the Above

From : nalinis@eth.net
To : saralee@intpharma.com
Cc : martin2000@intpharma.com
Subject: Meeting in India

Dear Sara Lee,

Thanks for your e-mail of 10th March 2004.

I confirm that

1. Draft agreement to be entered into with Wofhensten & Co is ready. Our legal advisors have vetted it.
2. Drawings of the electrical installation have been completed and are with the Chief Engineer now for final scrutiny.
3. A memo scheduling your meeting with the engineers at 6 pm on 17th March has been sent
4. The Bank has been alerted about your visit on the 17th. We shall get the relevant documents from the Bank on the 17th morning.

Kindly let me know if anything else needs to be done.

Regards,

(Nalini)

Request for Annual Accounts Statement

From : prabha432@hotmail.com
To : customercare@icicibank.com
(customercare@icicibank.com)
Subject: Savings Account/Existing Customer/
Complaint

Please send me the pass sheet (account statement) for the year 1.4.2003 to 31.3.2004 by e-mail at the earliest. I need it for audit purposes.

My e-mail id: prabha432@hotmail.com
Telephone no: +91-040-24330225

Thanks and regards,

(Prabha Radhakrishnan)

Reply to the Above

To : prabha432@hotmail.com
Subject: Re: Savings Account/Existing Customer/
Complaint

Dear Ms. Radhakrishnan,

We thank you for writing to us.

We are sending you the statement for the period 1st April, 2003 to 31st March, 2004 to your E-Mail Id registered in our banking records. The Statement is not sent across along with this mail. It is being sent across separately to your E-Mail Id registered with us.

Do write back to us for further assistance. We look forward to the opportunity to assist you.

Regards,

(Bharat Jaikishen)
Customer Service Officer

Reminder

To : customercare@icicibank.com
(customercare@icicibank.com)
Subject: Savings Account/Existing Customer/
Complaint

This is to remind you that I got the following e-mail from you a week ago in which you said that you will send me my accounts statement for the year ending 31.3.2004 soon. I have still not received it. I request you to send it to me asap.

My SB A/c no is 624003100567.

Thanks and regards,

(Prabha Radhakrishnan)

Sales Letters by E-mail

E-mail marketing is an affordable and increasingly targetable communications tool.

It gives you answers to important marketing questions very fast. Want to test a new offer or product price-point? Just send out a split-test e-mail and in no time the marketplace will tell you what to do.

E-mail is very flexible, and can be used it to meet all kinds of marketing challenges.

Points to Remember

- *Select Your Words Carefully*: With the increasing use of anti-spam software, even legitimate "opt-in" e-mails often get blocked. You need to choose words that prevent your e-mail from being filtered out. Never use the word "free" in a subject line.
- *Use A Casual Tone*: Nothing turns off a reader faster than stiff, formal language. You're not writing a college essay. Write your e-mail as if you were writing to a friend.
- *Use Short Sentences*: They're easier to read and sound more conversational than long sentences. Keep your sentences crisp and snappy. And use short words rather than long.
- *Use Bullets To Highlight Benefits*: People tend to scan e-mail rather than read every word. Bullet points

makes it easy for a reader to quickly catch key information on your product or service.

- *Use Testimonials*: Nothing builds confidence in your product quicker than comments from satisfied customers. Collect testimonials whenever you can. Include the customer's first and last name.
- *Hyperlinks Should Be Specific*: When you insert a link into your e-mail, make sure it takes the prospect to the specific into you referred to in your letter. Don't just link to your homepage and expect the prospect to search for your offer. Your response will drop significantly.
- *Offer An Incentive To Get The Prospect To Take Action Now*: It's not enough to publicize your product, you want the prospect to take action. At the end of your e-mail, tell the prospect what they should do next. Sign up for your newsletter? Visit your website? Download an e-book?

Five Mistakes To Avoid

- Using a weak "Subject" line

  It doesn't matter how compelling your e-mail offer is, or how brilliantly your message is written. If your subject line isn't working right, your letter will never get opened and your campaign will be a failure.

  Subject lines should be kept short. (Never exceed forty characters including spaces.) This means that every subject line must communicate extremely quickly and have a little punch.

- Burying your Web address.

  Write URL near the top of your message and not at the end of the letter. Some people don't want to read through all your copy. They're ready to click through right to your site.

- Failing to identify the reader's need quickly.

  Don't start your e-mail by enumerating every feature and benefit of your product. (You're not writing a datasheet!) Tell your prospects immediately that you have the perfect answer to their problem.

- Keeping the letter too short.

  Don't be afraid that your e-mail advertising letter won't get read. Prospects WILL read it if there is valuable information for them. The typical e-mail advertising letters run a good seven or eight paragraphs in length… often with bullets too. They work just fine.

  However, remember to write your URL in early, so that prospects can click through without reading every single word. Some people, though, like to read whatyou've got to say and will probably through the entire letter.

- Writing in a boring, flat style.

  Write in an interesting, attention getting manner. Imagine your prospect and talk to him.

Here are some examples of e-mail sales letters.

Selling A Book

Dear Physician,

Have you ever been sued for malpractice?

I hope not, because it can be a terrible, devastating experience.

If YOU are concerned about protecting your practice, your income, and your reputation, download our free report immediately. It's called "Five Steps You Can Take Now To Avoid A Malpractice Lawsuit" and you can download it free right now at:

http://www.abc.xyz

Selling Software

Subject: Shockmachine is FREE and it's AWESOME!

Hey, have we got something for YOU.

Shockmachine. Free. Now.

It's dynamite, and it's waiting for you at:

http://www.shockwave.com/xxx

Why does Shockmachine deserve a place on YOUR hard drive?

Well, first of all Shockmachine is free so it will cost you absolutely nothing.

Selling A Book

Sub : Software Marketing made Easy

Are you a software marketer?

Don't miss a terrific book written by my friend Rick Chapman. It's called:

"The Product Marketing Handbook For Software"

Rick's book covers every aspect of software marketing, from collateral to trade shows. Detailed stories examine actual software marketing successes and disasters. (You even get a free CD that includes a sample software marketing budget.) Don't miss it!

Go to http://www.Aegis-Resources.com and check it out.

14
APPENDIX–I

A GLOSSARY OF COMMERCIAL TERMS

Account	:	(1) a bookkeeping record of business transactions;
		(2) a customer or client
Accrue	:	to accumulate, as interest
Affidavit	:	a written oath
Amortization	:	the gradual paying off of a debt at regular intervals
Annuity	:	an investment that produces fixed yearly payment
Appraise	:	to evaluate
Appreciate	:	to increase in value
Arbitration	:	settlement of a dispute through a third party
Arrears	:	overdue debts
Assessment	:	evaluation for the purpose of taxation
Asset	:	something that is owned and of value
Assurance	:	a word of honour

Audit	:	(1) the checking of a business's financial record; (2) to check a business's financial records
Balance	:	(1) the difference between debits and credits; (2) to reconcile the difference between debits and credits
Bankruptcy	:	the legally declared state of being unable to pay debts
Brochure	:	a small hand-book
Brokerage	:	a business licensed to sell stocks and securities
Capital	:	money or property owned or used by a business
Collateral	:	property used as security for a loan
Commitments	:	obligations that have already been accepted
Compensation	:	payment, reimbursement
Consignment	:	shipment of goods to be paid for after sale/resale
Corporation	:	a business operating under a charter
Convenant	:	a sealed contract
Credit	:	(1) the entry of a payment in an account; (2) to enter a payment in an account

Data Processing	:	the handling of information; especially statistical information, by computer
Debit	:	(1) the entry of money owed in an account; (2) to enter money in an account
Debt	:	money owed
Deficit	:	a money shortage
Depreciate	:	to decrease in value
Direct mail	:	the sale of goods and services through the mail
Dividend	:	a share of profits divided among the stockholders of a corporation
Endorse	:	to sign the back of a cheque
Endowment	:	money given, as a bequest
Equity	:	the amount of money no longer owed on a purchase
Escrow	:	written evidence of ownership held by a third party until specified conditions are met
Executor	:	person named to carry out someone else's will
Exemption	:	money not subject to taxation
Expenditure	:	an amount of money spent
Fabrics	:	manufactured pieces of cloth
Facsimile	:	an exact copy
Fiscal	:	financial
Flexitime	:	a system of flexible work hours

Forfeiture	:	loss of property as a penalty for default
Franchise	:	a special right to operate a business granted by the government or a corporation
Gross	:	(1) total, before deductions; (2) to earn a certain amount before deductions; (3) the total before deductions; (4) twelve dozen
Hardware	:	the physical machinery of a computer
Indent	:	an order specially from other countries
Information Processing	:	the "marriage" of data processing and word processing
Input	:	data fed into a computer
Irrevocable	:	which cannot be altered
Insurance	:	the guarantee of compensation for specified loss
Interest	:	the fee charged for borrowing money
Inventory	:	an itemized list of property or merchandise
Investment	:	money put into a business or transaction to reap a profit
Invoice	:	a list of goods shipped
Journal	:	a written record of financial transaction

Lease : (1) a contract for renting property; (2) to rent or let

Ledger : a record book of debits and credits

Legacy : money or property left in a wall.

Liability : a debt or obligation

Lien : a claim on property as security against a debt

Liquidity : ability to turn assets into cash.

List price : retail price as listed in a catalogue

Margin : difference between cost and selling price

Markup : the percentage by which selling price is more than cost

Merger : the combining of two and more companies into one

Middleman : a businessperson who buys from a producer and resells at wholesales or retail in smaller quantities

Monetary : relating to money

Monopoly : exclusive control of a commodity or service

Mortgage : (1) the pledging of property as security for a loan; (2) to pledge property as security for a loan

Negotiable : transferable

Net	:	(1) an amount left after deductions; (2) to clear as profit
Networking	:	the establishing of business and professional contacts
Obsolescent	:	which become out of date
On a sliding scale	:	that varies with the quantity purchased
On time	:	observation of punctuality
Option	:	the right to act on an offer at an established price within a limited time
Out put	:	data provided by a computer
Overhead	:	the cost of running a business
Oversight	:	mistake, omission
Payable	:	owed
Personnel	:	employees, staff
Petty cash	:	money kept on hand for incidental purchases
Portfolio	:	the various securities held by an investor
Power of Attorney	:	the written right to legally represent another person
Premium	:	a payment, usually for an insurance policy
Productivity	:	rate of yield or output
Proprietor	:	owner
Prospective Customers	:	people who may purchase goods

Prospectus : a statement describing a business

Provisionally : temporarily

Proxy : authorization to vote for stockholder at a meeting

Quorum : the minimum number of members required to be present for the transaction of business at a meeting

Receivable : due

Reciprocate : to return the favour

Remittance : the sending of money in payment

Requisition : a written request for supplies

Resources : financial means

Resume : an outline of a job applicant's qualifications and experience

Rider : an amendment to a document

Royalty : a share of the profits from a book or invention paid to the author or patent holder

Salvage : items that are recoverable

Security : (1) funds or property held as a pledge of repayment;
(2) a stock or bond

Shareholder : one who owns shares of a corporation's stock

Software : the data and programming of a computer

Solvent : able to pay debts

Specification	:	a detailed description of items in use
Standardized	:	made of similar pattern or size
Standing credit	:	a credit of fixed amount
Stockholder	:	one who owns stock in a company
Subsidy	:	a monetary grant
Tabulated	:	arranged in the form of a list
Tariff	:	a tax on imports or exports
Telecommunications	:	high-speed communications via wire
Testimony	:	evidence
Turnaround time	:	time taken to complete a task
Trust	:	a monopoly formed by a combination of corporation
Unsolicited	:	that have not been asked for
Vitae	:	an outline of a job applicant's qualifications and experience, a resume
Word processing	:	the handling of narrative information by computer

APPENDIX–II
PAIRS OF TERMS OFTEN CONFUSED

Adverse	:	unfavourable
Averse	:	unwilling
Accede	:	to accept or to yield
Exceed	:	to surpass
Aid	:	to help or to assist
Aide	:	assistant
Already	:	previously
All ready	:	prepared
Answer	:	reply to a question, letter, etc.
Assent	:	consent
Ascent	:	rise
Bizarre	:	fantastic
Bazaar	:	a fair
Born	:	brought into existence
Borne	:	carried
Capitol	:	structure; building
Capital	:	metropolitan city
Causal	:	the product, a result
Casual	:	accidental
Complaisant	:	flattery
Complement	:	that which completes

Comprehensive	:	having large scope
Comprehensible	:	intelligible or understandable
Confident	:	sure; certain
Confidant	:	one in whom confidence is reposed
Connotation	:	a suggestive meaning
Denotation	:	explicit meaning
Continual	:	lasting with intermittent break
Continuous	:	lasting without intermittent break
Counselor	:	advisor
Councilor	:	member of a council
Device	:	tool
Devise	:	to think or to frame
Elicit	:	to obtain or to draw out
Illicit	:	illegal
Immigrate	:	movement to another country
Emigrate	:	to move from one's own country
Duel	:	a contest between two opponents
Dual	:	two fold
Equitable	:	fair
Equable	:	uniform; calm
Forbear	:	endure
Forgo	:	relinquish
Ingenious	:	skilful
Ingenuous	:	simple
Loath	:	reluctant
Loathe	:	detest
Maze	:	labyrinth

Maize : a corn

Official : authorized

Officious : meddlesome

Ordnance : military supplies

Ordinance : regulation

Pre-emptory : preferential

Peremptory : decisive

Pre-requisite : requirement

Personnel : a group of employed people

Personal : private

Prospective : view

Practical : suitable for use

Practicable : which can be practiced

Precedent : priority

Principle : tenet

Principal : chief

Sensuous : that appeals to the senses

Sewarage : the system of drainage for taking out filthy water

Specious : plausible

Spacious : roomy or having enough space

Stationary : which is fixed

Stationery : papers and other such articles

Statute : law

Statue : a piece of sculpture

Tortuous : twisting

Torturous : painful

APPENDIX–III
COMMERCIAL ABBREVIATIONS

A-1	:	first class
@	:	at the rate of
a.a.r	:	against all risks
abbrev.	:	abbreviation
abstr.	:	abstract
a/c; A/C; ac.	:	account
A.D.	:	Acknowledgement Due
a.d.	:	after date
admin.	:	administration
ad. val.	:	*ad valorem* (according to value)
ad.; advt.; advert.	:	advertisement
aftn.	:	afternoon
agcy.	:	agency
agt.	:	agent
alt.	:	alternate
amt.	:	amount
a/o	:	account of
art.	:	article
A/S	:	account sales or sales account
assn.; assoc.	:	association

asst.	:	assistant
bal.	:	balance
b.b.	:	bill book or bank book
B.C.	:	before Christ
d/a.	:	document against acceptance
d/d/	:	days after date/delivered
del.	:	deliver/delegate
dept., deptt	:	department
dis.	:	discount
Ditto	:	the same
div.	:	division/dividend
dk.	:	dock/dark
dks.	:	docks
do.	:	ditto (the same)
D/o	:	delivery order
doz.; dz.	:	dozen
d/p.	:	documents against payment
Dr.	:	doctor/debtor
d.s., d/s.	:	days after sight
dup.	:	duplicate
ea.	:	each
ed.	:	edited/edition/editor
EE.	:	errors expected
e.g.	:	*exempli gratia* (for example)
encl. (s)	:	enclosure (s)
E. & O.E	:	errors and omissions excepted
equit.	:	equivalent

esq.	:	esquire
est.	:	estimate/establish
et. Al.	:	*et alibate* (and elsewhere)
etc.	:	etcetera (and so forth and the rest)
et. Seq	:	et sequent (and the following)
ex.	:	example/from/exchange
exc.	:	exchange/exclusive
exec.	:	executive
ext.	:	extension
ex. div.	:	ex dividend (without dividend)
F.	:	Friday/fahrenheit
fac.; facs.	:	facsimile
f.a.s.	:	free alongside ship
f.d.	:	free docks (goods to be delivered)
fec.	:	fecit
fig.	:	figure
f.o.; fol.	:	folio
f.o.b	:	free on boar
flog.	:	foot-pound
F.O.R.	:	free on Rail
f.p.	:	foot-pound
f.p.a.	:	free particulars average (marine insurance)
gal./gall	:	gallon
gen.	:	general
gm.	:	gramme

Gr.	:	grains; grass
gr. wt.	:	gross weight
guar	:	guaranteed
Hon.	:	Honourable
hon.	:	honorary
H.P.	:	horse power
H.P.	:	hire purchase
Hr(s)	:	heat/height
i.c.	:	in charge
i.e.	:	*id est* (that is)
id.	:	*idem* (the same)
I.H.P	:	indicated horse power
imp.	:	imported/important
in.	:	inch
inc.	:	incorporation; incomplete/ including
incorp.	:	incorporated
in ex.	:	in extenso
inf.	:	information
ins.	:	insurance
inst.	:	instant (present month)
int.	:	interest
inv.	:	invoice
I/O.	:	inspecting order
I.O.U	:	I owe you
J.P.	:	Justice of the peace
Jr.	:	junior

Jt.	:	joint
k.	:	kilo
k.g.	:	kilogramme
k.m.	:	kilometre
k.o.	:	knock out
kt.	:	carat
kw.	:	kilowatt (s)
L or l	:	a pound (sterling)
lb.	:	a pound (weight)
L/C.	:	letter of credit
Lib.	:	library
Lim./ltd.,	:	limited
Lit.	:	litre
Ltd.	:	limited
lugg. Rail	:	goods train
m.	:	minute; month; metre
maj.	:	major
max.	:	maximum
m/d.	:	month after date
mdse.	:	merchandise
med.	:	medium
mem.	:	member
memo	:	memorandum
messrs	:	messieurs
mfg.	:	manufacturing
mfr.	:	manufacturer/manufacture
m.g.	:	milligram

mgr.	:	manager
mks.	:	marks
min.	:	minimum
misc.	:	miscellaneous
m.m.	:	milli metre
M.O.	:	money order
Mr.	:	Mister
M/s.	:	messrs
Mrs.	:	mistress
Ms.	:	manuscript
M/s.	:	months after sight
mos/mths	:	months
mts.	:	minutes
Mtge.	:	mortgage
n.	:	north/nitrogen
n.a.	:	not available/not applicable
N.B.	:	*nota bene* (mark well)
neg.	:	negative/negligible
nem. Con.	:	no one objecting
No.	:	number
nom. Cap.	:	nominal capital
nr.	:	near
n.s.	:	not specified
O.	:	order
o.a.	:	on account (of)
o.c.	:	overcharge, office copy
o.d.	:	on demand

O.I.G.S.	:	on India government service
o.s.	:	out of stock
oz.	:	ounce
p.	:	per or through
p.a.	:	per annum
p.c.	:	per cent
pcl.	:	parcel
pd.	:	paid
per ann.	:	per annum
pkg.	:	packing
P & L	:	profit and loss
P.N.	:	promissory note
P.O.	:	postal order/post office
pp.	:	pages
PP.	:	parcel post/particular person (telephone)
pro.	:	for
pro. Tem.	:	for the time being
prox.	:	proximo, next month
P.S.	:	postscript
P.T.O.	:	please turn over
q.v.	:	*quod vide* (which see)
qual.	:	quality.
Re.	:	refer or referring to
recd.	:	received
recpt.	:	receipt
regd.	:	registered

reg.	:	registered, regarding
retd.	:	retired/returned
R.P.	:	reply/paid
R.S.V.P.	:	respondez s'il vous plait (reply), if you please
S/d.	:	sight draft
Sec.	:	secretary/second
senr./Sr.	:	senior
S.N.	:	shipping note
Sq.	:	square
Sq.ft.	:	square foot
Sq.yd.	:	square yard
SS. /S/S	:	steamship
T.L.O.	:	total loss only
Tgm.	:	telegram
tr.	:	tare (weight)
ult.	:	ultimo (last month)
via.	:	by way of
V.P.L.	:	value payable letter
V.P.P.	:	value payable post
wt.	:	weight
w.e.f	:	with effect from
yd.	:	yard
yr.	:	year

Other Books on

WORD POWER SERIES

1. School Essays, Letters, Applications, and Stories For Higher Secondary Students **(New)**	110/-
2. Idiomatic English **(New)**	175/-
3. Effective English Comprehension Read Fast, Understand Better ! **(New)**	160/-
4. Latest Essays for College & Competitive Examinations **(New)**	150/-
5. Dictionary of New Words **(New)**	125/-
6. Art of English Conversation Speak English Fluently **(New)**	125/-
7. Teach Yourself English Grammar & Composition	125/-
8. Common & Uncommon Proverbs **(New)**	125/-
9. Effective Editing Help Yourself in Becoming a Good Editor **(New)**	150/-
10. Effective English A Boon for Learners **(New)**	125/-
11. Essays for Primary Classes	60/-
12. Essays for Junior Classes	60/-
13. Essays for Senior Classes	60/-
14. Dictionary of Synonyms and Antonyms	150/-
15. Dictionary of Idioms and Phrases	150/-
16. Common Phrases	125/-
17. How to Write & Speak Correct English	150/-
18. Meaningful Quotes	175/-
19. Punctuation Book	125/-
20. Top School Essays	110/-
21. How to Write Business Letters with CD	250/-
22. Everyday Grammar	150/-
23. Everyday Conversation	150/-
24. Letters for All Occasions	125/-

25. School Essays & Letters for Juniors	110/-
26. Common Mistakes in English	125/-
27. The Power of Writing	150/-
28. Learn English in 21 Lessons	125/-
29. First English Dictionary	125/-
30. Boost Your Spelling Power	125/-
31. Self-Help to English Conversation	125/-
32. The Art of Effective Communication	125/-
33. A Book of Proverbs & Quotations	110/-
34. Word Power Made Easy	160/-
35. English Grammar Easier Way	160/-
36. General English for Competitive Examinations	150/-
37. Spoken English	125/-
38. School Essays, Letters Writing and Phrases	125/-
39. How to Write & Speak Better English	125/-
40. Quote Unquote (A Handbook of Famous Quotations)	160/-
41. Improve Your Vocabulary	150/-
42. Common Errors in English	150/-
43. The Art of Effective Letter Writing	125/-
44. Synonyms & Antonyms	125/-
45. Idioms	125/-
46. Business Letters	125/-

Unit No. 220, Second Floor, 4735/22,
Prakash Deep Building, Ansari Road, Darya Ganj,
New Delhi - 110002, Ph.: 32903912, 23280047, 09811594448
E-mail: lotuspress1984@gmail.com, www.lotuspress.co.in

Notes